Coaching Leadership Teams

ENDORSEMENTS

As CEO you respond to a complex environment with essentially two items on your agenda – strategy and culture. Proper alignment of culture and strategy offers the organisation the best chance to flourish in this complex world. It is in this context that the book excites me. It affirms my belief that if the ethos (culture) of the organisation is not intact, it puts everything else at risk. The approach in this book offers a practical pathway to strategic and sustainable leadership practices hinging on the philosophy of an integrated ethos that permeates throughout the organisation.

—*Frik Landman, CEO, USB Executive Development*

This book provides a narrative based on the author's work in one organisation over a number of years, with others as added weight. This provides a cogent story, creating a clear insight into her team coaching model. I recommend it to all interested in the field as an enlightening account of real value.

—*Professor David A Lane, Professional Development Foundation and Middlesex University*

Companies and organisations without a well-aligned and common "way forward" will have a hard time being successful over time. Dr Salomé van Coller-Peter has in this book successfully managed to describe – in a concrete way – how to create such an alignment. This book will be helpful to all leaders of organisations, big or small, and stimulate their organisational thinking and how to get their culture aligned.

—*Jan-Ola Andersson, Deputy Divisional Manager: ÅF Industry AB, Malmö, Sweden.*

Management coaching has grown into a mature and credible vehicle for enhanced personal and organisational performance. At USB, our coaching programme is backed by solid research that brings actual business benefit. This book by Dr Salomé van Coller-Peter, is highly recommended as a prime example of integrating theory, narrative, and practice for the good of the client.

—*Piet Naude, Director: University of Stellenbosch Business School (USB)*

Every year organisations throw enormous amounts of money at training and change programmes with spectacularly limited results … Why?

Typically, certain organisational levels (not teams) attend with little time and support for on-the-job application from leaders and colleagues. There is limited measurement and reward for new learning, as the old culture subtly dictates what and how things really get done – all of which leaves disillusioned learners permanently pregnant without delivering.

Salome's book offers a 'must-read' holistic way of addressing these shortfalls and offers a proven, practical alternative to Sustainable Performance.

—*Guy Charlton, consultant, author, speaker, coach*

Salomé has crafted a book of great practical insight which also contributes to lifting the art and skill of coaching in general and team coaching in particular to new heights. Her many years as a coach together with her experience and contributions in designing and running a Master's degree in coaching brings theory and practice together in an energising manner. It is a pleasure to read something on coaching that is both so accessible and robust.

Christo Nel, Director: The Village Leadership Consulting & Programme Director of International MBA and Executive MBA at —Nyenrode Business Universiteit in the Netherlands

"The field of coaching needs to urgently link its work to creating culture change and more value-based work in and between organisations. In this book Salomé van Coller has made a great contribution to this endeavour with theory, guidance and detailed case studies."

—*Peter Hawkins, Bath Consultancy Group*

"Salomé Van Coller-Peter has made an immensely valuable contribution to coaches and team leaders with her practical, accessible advice supported by case study examples. The appeal of her writing is the authenticity and relevance of the account of her personal growth and professional development as a coach. Her particular focus on consolidating team values in support of highly motivated performance will no doubt make this book will an essential handbook for coaches, managers of teams, and those interested in the hands-on step-by-step process of achieving excellence in teams."

—*Dr Dorrian Aiken, Executive Leadership Development Coach*

"Salomé van Coller has been involved in coaching in South Africa from the start. Her efforts at Stellenbosch Business School have resulted in the establishment of a leading Master's programme in coaching that enjoys many accolades. Salomé has also maintained her own coaching and consulting practice over the years providing services to many companies. In this book, she illustrates her extensive experience and expertise in a very personal way, providing insight into the workings of a practising coach and consultant working with leadership teams in the field today. In particular, she demonstrates in detail how to deliver coaching services using the case of Viking Enterprises which will be a valuable lens for students in understanding how coaching leadership teams can contribute to performance."

—*Marc Simon Kahn, Global Head of HR at Investec, and author of Coaching on the Axis.*

Coaching Leadership Teams

Getting organisational culture aligned

Dr Salomé van Coller-Peter

2015

Copyright © Knowres Publishing and Dr Salomé van Coller-Peter

All reasonable steps have been taken to ensure that the contents of this book do not, directly or indirectly, infringe any existing copyright of any third person and, further, that all quotations or extracts taken from any other publication or work have been appropriately acknowledged and referenced. The publisher, editors and printers take no responsibility for any copyright infringement committed by an author of this work.

Copyright subsists in this work. No part of this work may be reproduced in any form or by any means without the written consent of the publisher or the author.

While the publisher, editors and printers have taken all reasonable steps to ensure the accuracy of the contents of this work, they take no responsibility for any loss or damage suffered by any person as a result of that person relying on the information contained in this work.

First published in 2015

ISBN: 978-1-86922-579-7
eISBN: 978-1-86922-580-3 (PDF eBook)

Published by Knowres Publishing
P O Box 3954
Randburg
2125
Republic of South Africa

Tel: (011) 706-6009
Fax: (011) 706-1127
E-mail: orders@knowres.co.za
Website: www.kr.co.za

Printed and bound: Mega Digital (Pty) Ltd, Parow Industria, Cape Town
Typesetting, layout and design: Cia Joubert, cia@knowres.co.za
Cover design and art work: Marlene de Villiers, marlene@knowres.co.za
Editing and proofreading: Jill Bishop, jill.bishop@absamail.co.za
Project management: Cia Joubert, cia@knowres.co.za

*The Viking symbol on the cover represents balance. The four outer circles symbolize the four elements: earth, fire, water and air. The middle circle unites all the components with a goal to reach a balance between all four elements or energies.

ACKNOWLEDGEMENT

My heartfelt appreciation goes to:

My Creator and the universe for the courage, strength and grace that I have been blessed with to finish this book

My parents, who gave me unconditional love and support through all the years of my life, including the finances to get qualified in something that I was passionate about

Arne, my husband, and Leila, my daughter, for their patience, love and support through all the years of studying and months of writing

My siblings, friends and colleagues for their love, support and much-needed nudges (some gentler than others)

Dr Derrick Morton-Achmad, Professor Eon Smit and Amanda Matthee for their support with the proofreading and editing of this book

The students of Coaching at USB, with whom I have had the privilege to learn and hone my thinking, doing and being

Wilhelm Crous, my first career mentor, for believing in this book

Dr Sunny Stout-Rostron for the smart foreword. She succinctly captured the essence and mood of the manuscript. I truly appreciate your abundance.

TABLE OF CONTENTS

Foreword	vii
About the author	x
Preface	xi
Acronyms	xiv

CHAPTER 1: Making a coaching footprint 1

Introduction	1
Homogenous work teams	2
What is professional coaching?	4
A journey of self-discovery	5
Wisdom, learning and reflections	5
Coaching for performance	6
How my coaching journey unfolded	7
The coach's values: How do they emerge in the coaching?	8
Client perceptions – the only reality	9
Developing a signature presence	10
My team coaching work	11
Conclusion	11

CHAPTER 2: Values, once agreed and shared, promote team performance 13

Introduction	13
How do values become shared?	13
Culture and its role in business decisions	14
Value creation facilitates long-term gains through shared leadership practice	16
The value questions	18
The leadership alignment challenge	18
The importance of cultural alignment	19
Aligning subcultures and their values	20
The impact of subcultures	20
Conclusion	21

CHAPTER 3: How all that we learn, experience and believe shapes our coaching approach 23

Introduction	23
The process of cultural renewal	25
Shared concerns	25

i

Contracting	26
Does a handshake indicate mutual consent?	26
My journey through the corporate world	29
Assessment centres	29
Cohesive work teams	29
Coaching and the transfer of skills	30
My personal coaching model	30
Phase 1: Exploring a partnership	31
Phase 2: Forming a pact	32
Phase 3: Coaching with zest	32
Other modalities of value	33
Neuro-linguistic programming	33
Force field analysis	34
The six thinking hats	35
Questioning frameworks	36
Mindfulness	36
Phase 4: Implementation and reflection	37
Phase 5: Recognising, appreciating and checking out	37
Learning theories that shaped my coaching approach	39
Conclusion	41

CHAPTER 4: Getting started at Viking Enterprises — 43

Introduction	43
Confidentiality and name changes	43
Communication with Viking Enterprises	43
The start of a partnership with Viking Enterprises	44
The challenge of Viking Enterprises	45
Viking Enterprises' subcultures and the challenges they posed	45
Travelling to the first key meeting	46
The interview	47
Questions on the company status	47
Questions on the company culture and values	48
Objectives agreed	50
Conclusion	51

CHAPTER 5: Coaching: Aligning culture with strategy — 53

Introduction	53
The coaching mandate	53
Stakeholders and beneficiaries	54

Coaching sessions	54
Making meaning through reflection	55
Values and relationships	55
Agreeing on the relevance of the process	56
Aligning culture and strategy	56
Leadership styles and cultures	57
Future state and environment	58
Journalling my findings	59
A new vision statement	59
Setting and planning team goals	61
Questionnaire: Harrison and Stokes	62
Conclusion	62

CHAPTER 6: Setting the key milestones — 65

Introduction	65
Why some initiatives fail	65
Milestone 1: Reaching agreement on the coaching process	68
Milestone 2: Developing an organisational strategy	70
Milestone 3: Sharing perceptions	71
The application of the organisational culture survey	71
Survey results of the executive team and the representative group	72
Establishing the main points of agreement	72
Milestone 4: Determining variances between current and preferred cultures	72
Milestone 5: Coaching for improved leadership practice	73
Milestone 6: Setting goals to facilitate the preferred culture	76
Conclusion	78

CHAPTER 7: Meeting the key milestones through a combined coaching process — 79

Introduction	79
Milestone 1: Reaching agreement on the coaching process	79
What the team wanted	80
Coaching as the vehicle	80
Confidentiality	81
Milestone 2: Developing an organisational strategy	81
Milestone 3: Sharing perceptions	82
Comparison: Survey results of the executive team and representative group	82
Establishing the main issues of agreement	83
Milestone 4: Determining variances between old and new cultures	84
Step 1: Identify the most significant variances	84

Step 2: Agree on critical leadership practices	86
Milestone 5: Coaching for improved leadership practice	86
Round 1: Some coaching outcomes	87
A comprehensive sales strategy	87
Transparent and inclusive team decision-making	88
Sharing of information	89
The phenomenological approach to team coaching	90
Round 2: Some coaching outcomes	90
Strategic alignment	90
Cooperation: Project- and consultancy-oriented business units	92
A strategy for project management	93
Round 3: Some coaching outcomes	93
More attention to people management	93
Better-managed meetings	94
Individual member reflections: Improvements	94
Round 4: Some coaching outcomes	95
Development in competence	95
An induction programme	96
Milestone 6: Setting goals to facilitate the preferred culture	96
Conclusion	99
CHAPTER 8: Success for Viking Enterprises!	**101**
CHAPTER 9: Adapting the coaching process to achieve alignment in varying contexts	**105**
Introduction	105
Case Study 1	105
Case Study 2	109
My own learning	112
Concluding comments	113
CHAPTER 10: Learning and reflections on ethics in coaching	**115**
Introduction	115
What are ethics?	115
Whose ethics code to follow?	115
Core coaching values	116
Inclusivity	116
Dignity	116
Integrity	117

Whose ethics are relevant?	117
Ethical challenges during team-coaching projects	117
Conclusion	121

CHAPTER 11: A snapshot of my most profound personal learning and reflections to date — 123

Introduction	123
Learning and reflection	123
Reflection is a form of mental processing	124
Storytelling as a form of reflection	125
Key learning about the use of coaching to discern organisational culture	126
The use of a questionnaire to determine current and preferred organisational culture	127
Team coaching	127
Individual coaching	129
How to ensure ethical conduct throughout coaching processes	129
Using a project approach	130
The use of recordings, transcripts and reflection	130
An objective look at the feasibility of this coaching project	130
Credibility with the client organisation	130
Complicating factors	131
Difference in values	131
Language differences	131
Timeframe	131
Playing multiple roles	131
Lessons for institutions considering coaching initiatives to change culture and values	132
Conclusion	132

APPENDICES — 133

Appendix A: Example of agreement with Viking Enterprises	133
Appendix B: Complete balanced scorecard for Viking Enterprises	138
Appendix C: Code of conduct	143
Appendix D: New performance management form for Viking Enterprises	144
ENDNOTES	149
REFERENCES	150
INDEX	154

List of tables

Table 3.1 Four stages of the conscious competence theory _____ 28
Table 6.1 Summary of planned sequencing for priority challenge practices _____ 75
Table 7.1 Significant variances between current and preferred cultures
         as seen by the executive team_____ 85
Table 8.1 Score sheet_____ 102

List of figures

Figure 3.1 Basic force field analysis _____ 34
Figure 3.2 The Six Thinking Hats of Edward de Bono_____ 36
Figure 3.3 A graphic representation of the author's coaching model___ 38
Figure 5.1 How a business strategy is decided _____ 57
Figure 5.2 Mapping out the business environment _____ 58
Figure 5.3 The market environment _____ 60
Figure 6.1 The milestones reached by Viking Enterprises _____ 77
Figure 7.1 The balanced scorecard pro forma used by Viking Enterprises _____ 91
Figure 7.2 Force field analysis of Viking Enterprises after setting milestones and
         reaching agreement _____ 99
Figure 11.1 Illustrating the differences between facilitation and team coaching____ 128

FOREWORD by DR SUNNY STOUT-ROSTRON

Dr Salomé van Coller, as befitting a key driver of postgraduate academic programmes in management coaching, has given us an accessible story, where we can follow her own learning and development as we discover important insights relevant to all coaching practitioners. Her new book is enlightening, insightful and a welcome addition to the knowledge base for organisational coaching. What is particularly refreshing is her light, narrative touch with useful, practical examples – from which we can learn how to use Salome's Team Alignment Coaching model.

Salome's message to the reader is clear and absolutely crucial: "It is only once we have developed an approach true to ourselves that we are able to offer consistently good coaching. In so doing, we strengthen the image of coaching as a responsible and sustainable development practice". Her book provides the reader with a mixed-method approach – using training, facilitation and coaching to show how the coaching process can help clients develop sustainable leadership practices within their new, preferred culture.

The core of the book is the detailed analysis of a major organisation, Viking Enterprises in Sweden, with which Salome worked over several years. As a team coach she helped develop the organisation's new leadership culture. We discover the progress of the team as Viking Enterprises moved from a control- and role-orientation environment to one characterised by achievement and support. Through her work, Salome's model began to take shape: from the early beginnings of using a questionnaire as a pre- and postmeasure of the culture, through the development of an organisational strategy, to individual and team coaching processes as they evolved.

With two other case studies, Salome demonstrates to the reader how her team alignment coaching process can become your own. Her key learnings with each organisational team intervention included the findings that the newly empowered individual feels encouraged and trusted to try out his or her new learning; that transfer of learning to the workplace is facilitated by the leader/manager of the work unit; and that there is an **immediate** need for implementation of the new learning.

Team coaching is helpful in boosting the cohesion and effectiveness of functional teams within companies. According to Salome, it is important not to confuse the team coaching process with training, facilitation and individual coaching – and to ensure that if there is no strategy in place that a new strategy is facilitated by a different consultant prior to beginning the team coaching process. In this way, the team members are not confused by the team coach constantly explaining the different hats he or she is wearing.

Throughout the book, Salome reiterates in different ways that "coaches will not be true to themselves and others if they do not do some deep and honest reflection about themselves and their practices". Her greatest insight in the work she describes is that "similar team values lead to stronger collective action in the workplace, and that they produce little if any dysfunctional conflict – and the need to include **values and culture** in the development of a strategic focus".

I have always advocated that any leadership or management development strategy which includes individual and/or team coaching needs to be aligned with the client organisation's performance and business strategy. This includes the required behaviours, values, capabilities and competences which have been identified for a wide range of leadership and management roles. In this book, Salome also advocates that values, once agreed and shared, promote team performance. She firmly believes that "personal values, leadership values and team values can all be embraced consciously, becoming tools that allow the choice of new behaviours, helping to bring about meaning and value to one's life. However, there needs to be alignment among the values that an individual declares, whether they are personal or professional values, and those values representing the peer group or team."

Salome strongly suggests that alignment of personal, leadership and team values – to be embraced consciously – must be aligned with the self. And only then can they become tools for change in behaviour, bringing about new meaning in one's life. Salome says that it is this alignment with self that has become the essence of her purpose for coaching.

Team coaching can help new leaders and their teams manage all aspects of transition, transformation and change. But in order to do this the coach also needs to have an in-depth understanding of organisational systems – seeing the coaching intervention from a systems perspective, and understanding the need for "structure" in the interaction between coach, individual client, team and the organisational system. I have argued strongly in my own work that a danger of not understanding the "system" in which the client operates is that the coach risks becoming another part of that system.

As a business coach, whether working with individuals or teams, you are helping your clients to understand the complexity of the environment in which they work. Team coaching is becoming more affordable than individual executive coaching, and ensures that the team is working together in alignment with organisational values and goals. Because we are still in the beginning stages of researching exactly what "team coaching" comprises, Salome's book is a stimulating addition to the scant literature on the topic.

Salome's work has taken her to Africa, the UK, the US and Scandinavia. One of her more important conclusions is the need for the coach "to accept the clients for who they are" and how crucial that is when their "backgrounds differ from the coach culturally, spiritually, socially and intellectually". As she so rightly says, "the clients' perceptions serve as the essential beginning for meaningful conversations".

The proof that her model works is that in the example of Viking Enterprises, her main case study, she was invited back after four years and discovered a culture of high performance and support. The company "had had its best financial year since the introduction of the coaching intervention." Her client said that the "upturn was a result of their focus on their preferred culture and leadership practices" and a shift from a control- and role-oriented culture to one characterised by performance and support.

You will find Salome's research suggestions practical and thought-provoking – and a useful guide to thinking through your own team coaching model.

Dr Sunny Stout-Rostron
August 2015

ABOUT THE AUTHOR

Dr Salomé van Coller-Peter is an industrial psychologist registered with the Health Professions Council of South Africa and is also an internationally qualified professional coach. She has been involved in the personal coaching and mentoring of executives in a variety of industries and on different continents for the past 20 years. She is also involved in training professional coaches and in setting ethical standards for coaches and mentors in South Africa.

As a consultant, Salomé focuses on transformation within organisations by ensuring that leadership teams are aligned in terms of their strategic focus and the collective values that inform their personal behaviour and leadership style.

She graduated from Middlesex University in the UK with a doctorate in Coaching. Her pioneering work in the area of alignment within executive teams has been published both locally and internationally and forms the essence of this book.

As a faculty member of the University of Stellenbosch Business School (USB), Salomé has developed an MPhil in Management Coaching (a first for the African continent) and still heads this programme together with a formidable team of academics. In both 2013 and 2014, this programme was rated as the best Master's Programme in Africa (Human Resources and Leadership category) by Eduniversal.

Salomé also focuses her energy on the development of young entrepreneurs from previously disadvantaged communities and on strengthening ethics and professionalism within the coaching fraternity.

Her core belief is that individuals have the innate ability to motivate themselves and to find answers to their own questions or situations, and that coaching is the vehicle through which this can be facilitated.

PREFACE

This book is for those leaders, team leaders, coaching practitioners and organisational effectiveness specialists who want to successfully manage coaching projects focusing on teams and alignment. More specifically, this book provides you with a mixed-method approach to coaching. Team coaching and one-on-one coaching are combined to facilitate agreement in terms of the strategy and culture of an organisation. Best of all, the case studies in this book show how the coaching process helped clients to translate their preferred culture into leadership practices, which they embraced and incorporated into their balanced scorecards (BSCs) and daily activities. In doing so, they shifted completely to their consciously chosen culture in approximately four years.

In chapter 1, I relate personal experiences that confirm my belief that the alignment of first values and then conduct leads to sustainable change. Those who have the passion and impetus to increase the performance of their organisations or teams authentically will find this chapter useful. I also share with you how my coaching journey began, how I distilled my values as a coach and why I think signature presence is key to having meaningful coaching conversations.

Chapter 2 speaks of the clarity and focus that shared values and organisational culture give to decision-making and commitment to action. It explores some questions about values with leaders at all levels, including what it means to wear values openly and to leave behind a legacy. It also shares how the agreed and expressed values of a team can become the barometer of the organisation and, lastly, how coaching can act as a support mechanism to make values practical.

In chapter 3, I share my purpose for coaching, the multiple perspectives that inform me and the framework that I use when coaching one-on-one. I highlight my beliefs around cultural change and how these are embedded in good, solid learning theory, informed by systems thinking. Come with me on a short journey through life and the corporate world, and see the impact of coaching on the development of a personal signature presence in coaching for alignment.

If your coaching spans cultures and even countries, you will appreciate chapter 4. This chapter defines organisational culture and its role in business, and it explains why shared leadership practices facilitate long-term gains. It then moves to the story of how and where I met my clients, the questions I posed to find out what they really wanted and how I subsequently contracted with them in project fashion.

In the last part of the book I share with you how my learning was honed through subsequent cases and projects. But for now, here is a story-telling approach to how I established a relationship, reached agreement and contracted with and served a company that, for reasons of confidentiality, I will call Viking Enterprises.

In initial discussions with Viking Enterprises about a potential alignment process, they expressed the need to revisit their strategic plan since they felt that it was outdated. They realised that my approach to alignment was that "the focus of core business" had to be very clear in order to make viable and relevant decisions about how to do business. The Viking Enterprises needed to renew their business strategy first. For this reason, chapter 5 is devoted to the process we went through to distil a new strategy and to plan the process of aligning the culture with the strategy.

Oops! It turned out that Viking Enterprises did not have a strategy, and here I was, ready and willing to support them in their quest to agree on a common organisational culture. This did not sit well with me, so I took a step back. I realised that if I wanted to be true to my beliefs, I needed to help them agree on a strategy first (what they were in the business to do) and then decide on the culture (how they agreed on doing it). Therefore, chapter 5 is devoted to the process we went through to distil a new strategy and to plan the process of aligning the culture with the strategy.

Chapters 6 and 7 have a distinct project management orientation, since these sections represent the culture-alignment project I have mentioned before. The reasons for doing it in project fashion were that my clients were mostly engineers and that good project management is always the fall-back method for a right-brainer like me. For students of coaching and leadership, perhaps this is of value as a way to manage their own projects, whether these are in research or practice. Chapter 6 tells you how the milestones of the project were set and chapter 7 explains how these were met.

Success for Viking Enterprises! Chapter 8 is dedicated to the success that the company achieved as a result of their dedication to the process of aligning their culture with their strategy and agreeing on leadership practices that facilitated alignment, followed by group and individual coaching to ensure sustainable shift, both for themselves and among team members.

Progress is inevitable when you strive to apply and hone existing processes. In chapter 10 I share two more case studies where the combined coaching approach previously introduced was adapted into processes that suited the particular clients' needs for alignment. The learning to be gathered from this chapter is that such processes need to be flexible to accommodate not just the needs but also the character of your clients, their view of coaching, their readiness to be coached and the readiness of their environments to accommodate and implement changed ways of thinking, doing and being.

Coaches will not be true to themselves and others if they do not do some deep and honest reflection about themselves and their practices. The last two chapters in this book represent my personal learning about how to do and be, through having learnt how not to do and be. This is a snapshot in time of my coaching practice in the particular area of team alignment.

Thank you for picking up, perhaps buying and then perhaps even reading this book!

Salomé van Coller-Peter

ACRONYMS

BSC	Balanced scorecard
ICF	International Coach Federation
Comensa	Coaches and Mentors of South Africa
CBC	Cognitive Behavioural Coaching
EI	Emotional intelligence
EU	European Union
MD	Managing Director
NLP	Neuro-linguistic programming
ROLI	Return on Learning Investment
SWOT	Strengths, weaknesses, opportunities and threats
2IC	Second-in-command

Chapter 1

MAKING MY COACHING FOOTPRINT

INTRODUCTION

I am a professional executive coach. My primary aim when coaching is to facilitate personal ownership by the client, increase self-awareness and establish a strong foundation that supports personal and long-term organisational goals. Thus, the message I put out to my clients is: Focus on the long-term view, focus on what is right for you and not just on what seems good, and focus especially on building a legacy for the community you serve and by whom you are served.

For the past two decades, I have been consulting to organisations on their strategic planning, transformation and performance management, and my roles in this have varied. At times, I was the outsider consultant; in other settings, I formed part of the executive team. My feelings about the coaching outcomes varied too. At first, my reaction to success was to be pleased; later the same achievement brought disappointment. This happened when executive teams (even the ones I had been part of) returned to the drawing board to strategise instead of implementing plans that had seemed both brilliant and well-conceived. Why did that happen – such reluctance to act decisively after meticulous planning?

A noticeable trend in South Africa before, during and even after the turn of the century has been vacillation between the centralisation and decentralisation of operations. The reasons have never been clear to me but there is a pattern to shifts like these. After implementation comes the inevitable retrenchment of labour, and then barely months later I see reports of the re-employment of large numbers of staff. It made little sense to me every time.

What had been the point of the restructuring? What could I be missing? Well, ever since the year 2002, I have posed these questions to the leaders and managers I coached. They, too, were at a loss to explain what I was missing. On surveying the habits of nearly 200 executives and reflecting upon the results, it seemed safe to conclude that not all the leaders had bought into the restructuring process – some lacked deep commitment to the outcomes.

It took some intense coaching for those managers to grasp their own reasons for failing to implement decisions and to execute the actions expected of them.

By working through my own coaching reflections and those of my clients, I concluded that only when people are guided by their own conscience are they highly motivated to act decisively and to decide when they should and can do so. By this I mean that only when the expected actions of such leaders are in line with their own personal value systems are they enabled to do what needs to be done. When they do act, they show astonishing conviction and energy.

I found the converse to be true too. When leaders are expected to display behaviour or execute decisions at odds with what drives them or makes them feel proud, or what they are comfortable with, they tend to balk at the starting block. They then seek reasons to do more planning, stall or even just ignore what is required of them.

I felt my first pangs of discomfort with organisational culture when I worked in the banking sector in the role of industrial psychologist. At that time my company had just gone through a merger with a number of other financial institutions, and in that process the differences between the company with the power and the ones forced into the merger became starkly obvious.

On the one hand, the dominant company is often characterised by clumsy processes with many levels of decision-making and high levels of control, all of which profess to mitigate risk. On the other hand, the smaller companies typically have fewer levels of decision-making, with fewer control procedures and an easier flow of communication in many directions. The latter attributes are patently positive ones in any quest for long-term growth. Yet little effort is made to maintain the good practices of the smaller companies. It became clear to me that those who wield the power get to decide just how things must be done in the new scheme of things.

Later, I tell you more about the personal value base that guides my behaviour as coach, and how I saw it compromised by the new organisational culture in which I found myself.

HOMOGENOUS WORK TEAMS

I derived much satisfaction from working as an executive member of the human resources (HR) and change management division in a large multinational. In that role I was tasked with the challenge of aligning teams of people who had diverse business cultures. From my position within an international organisation that employed people from a variety of cultures, I noticed something significant. In fact, it leapt out at me. I saw a much lower level of conflict between team members from similar cultural backgrounds, compared with those members who hailed from diverse cultures. The observation became significant when I later helped to integrate my company's four independent business units into one focused organisation.

The restructuring process of merging the four business units saw a new combination of work teams put in place, teams that were based not only on skill but also on cultural grounds. The teams moved unusually fast from the team **forming** phases to the final **performing** phases. Levels of internal conflict and role confusion were negligible. The new team arrangements facilitated better group cooperation and ultimately yielded improved levels of performance and client service. Profit margins rose in tandem.

Upon reflecting on these experiences described above, I have come to realise firstly that like cultures tend to adopt like value systems, and secondly that culture may not be the only determining factor in improved group performance. A tiny seed planted itself in my mind. The seedling it became moved me to dig deeply into the hypothesis that similar team values lead to stronger collective action in the workplace. Moreover, they produce little, if any, dysfunctional conflict. That was a breakthrough in my thinking.

During my project management experiences in Scandinavia, which lasted six years, I furthered my studies in the area of coaching and conducted the research for my doctorate in an engineering company. That period of my life is significant for this book. It was during the three and a half years of my doctoral research that I learnt some of my most valuable lessons on how to help teams of people discover their collective values. I found ways to translate those lessons into actions and learnt how to integrate newly practised behaviours into measurable activities.

All outcomes were carefully linked to the strategic intent and direction of the organisation. I took the learning from those years and applied it within different companies on other continents, and I share that learning with you in the last chapter of this book. The significance of my learning during this period and my own reflections on ethics are found in chapter 10.

In this book, I tell you about my journey to becoming a professional coach. I also share the profound lessons that I have learnt as I reflected in the moment about personally meaningful "aha!"s and "oh no!"s. Travel with me. Let my journey speak to those of you enamoured with coaching, those planning to get on board, or those in full pursuit of your own passion.

To the student of coaching, I want you to know that this journey offers a unique approach to coaching and will provide helpful direction in the development of your own coaching framework and model.

Are you addressing company culture right now or do you need to do so in the near future? The main case study presented in this book is one of the very first to include a combination of team coaching and one-on-one coaching. That is why it is unique. It achieved a complete culture shift within a medium-sized business in just three years and has since worked equally well in bigger organisations.

The complete case study is described in chapters 6 and 7 of this book, with a clear process map and the tools required for roll-out in your own environment.

I do hope you find my style of writing easy to read, and I hope too that you enjoy the coaching journey as much as I have done. It had its harrowing times, of course, but the overall experience remains satisfying to this day.

WHAT IS PROFESSIONAL COACHING?

At this point, I pose the question: What is professional coaching? For now, I give you my **amended** version of the definition used by the International Coach Federation (ICF):[1]

> Professional coaching is an ongoing professional relationship that helps people produce extraordinary results in their lives, careers, businesses or organisations. Through the process of coaching, clients deepen their learning, improve their performance, and enhance their quality of life.

The definition below is the one that appears on the ICF website:

> ICF defines coaching as partnering with clients in a thought-provoking and creative process that inspires them to maximize their personal and professional potential, which is particularly important in today's uncertain and complex environment. Coaches honor the client as the expert in his or her life and work and believe every client is creative, resourceful and whole. Standing on this foundation, the coach's responsibility is to:
>
> - Discover, clarify, and align with what the client wants to achieve.
> - Encourage client self-discovery.
> - Elicit client-generated solutions and strategies.
> - Hold the client responsible and accountable.

The definition below is that of the professional association of Coaches and Mentors of South Africa (Comensa), taken from its website:

> The professional association of Coaches and Mentors of South Africa (Comensa) defines coaching as 'a professional, collaborative and outcomes-driven method of learning that seeks to develop an individual and raise self-awareness so that he

or she might achieve specific goals and perform at a more effective level'. Coaching is as much about the way things are done as about what is done. Coaching delivers results in large measure because of the supportive relationship between the coach and the participant, and the means and style of communication used by the coach.[2]

In each coaching session, the client chooses the focus of conversation while the coach listens and contributes observations and questions. This interaction creates clarity and moves the client into action. Coaching accelerates the client's progress by providing greater focus and awareness of choice. It concentrates on where that client is at a specific point, and what he or she is willing to do to get where he or she wants to be in the future. The client is left in little doubt about the direction ahead, and confidence in the coach is created from the outset.

Professional coaches recognise that results are really a function of the client's intentions, choices and actions, supported by the coach's efforts and application of the appropriate coaching process. As coach, my key areas of responsibility to the client are:

- Discover, clarify and align with what the client wants to achieve.
- Elicit client-generated solutions and strategies.
- Hold the client responsible and accountable.
- Encourage the client to embark on self-discovery learning.

A JOURNEY OF SELF-DISCOVERY

Substantial change in behaviour, unless forced upon us, usually comes from within ourselves. I have found that people learn best by reflecting on personal experiences and on the practices employed in gaining that experience. Hence, most people learn best by self-discovery, which is a form of self-directed learning that occurs largely outside formal education structures. People engage in self-discovery mainly when they voluntarily pursue informal problem-solving behaviour to seek out information or learning opportunities. Any experienced coach will tell you that the self-discovery approach to learning becomes more effective when facilitated by a process of reflection, which may or may not include the guidance of a coach or mentor.

WISDOM, LEARNING AND REFLECTIONS

This book gives you an account of my journey as a coach over a period of 12 years. At some point I found true personal meaning and purpose in coaching both individuals and teams. I therefore include an honest account of lessons learnt, as well as professional and personal reflections on my journey. I found that continuous learning lies at the very foundation of coaching. Hence, the teaching and learning processes are ongoing for both the coach and the client. That is why I love this quote: "It's never really over and the fat lady seldom gets to sing".[3]

This chapter also touches on some of my learning in corporate business and the growing need I saw for including values and culture in the strategic focus and how we agree to do business. My enduring passion remains aligning key activities with the organisational culture and the values underpinning that culture. That passion embraces a reflection on shared values, shared concerns and a systems thinking approach within leadership and work teams. These three concepts are briefly explained in the next paragraph.

Companies gain strength and prosperity when their employees uphold values that are shared throughout the organisation. Values become shared when reinforced and lived out by all, especially the leaders of the organisation. The concept of systems thinking may be defined as the process of understanding how things relate to one another and influence one another within a whole. This understanding is achieved by focusing on the interrelatedness, interdependence and relationships between systemic components.[4] The concept of shared concern is the starting point for meaningful coaching. It is a sense that both the client and the coach are on the same page in understanding the objectives of the coaching relationship and have the same understanding of the challenges or opportunities facing the client.

All those elements combine to align thoughts and behaviours towards common corporate goals and objectives. My evolution into a professional coach was therefore a natural progression given my passion, education and training, and my background as an industrial psychologist with an understanding of human behaviour in the workplace.

COACHING FOR PERFORMANCE

Coaching is a powerful developmental tool for any leader or team that aims to enhance work performance. It is highly effective in helping individuals to access untapped potential and underutilised strengths. Whatever the type of coaching I undertake, whether life coaching, executive leadership or team coaching, the process remains a transformational and dynamic one.

Our perceptions, beliefs and personal value systems are rooted in our very foundation. They all help to shape our philosophy about life and the people in it. They guide the way we approach situations. They also guide what I hope to achieve through my coaching. At one stage on my learning path in professional coaching, I found my own purpose and process for coaching becoming clearly defined. The time seemed right to test how its application could bring about outcomes relevant to the client. It was equally important that the purpose and process had to be meaningful to me, and to ensure this I developed a model that depicted my coaching process with its interrelated parts. Chapter 3 explains my own personal coaching framework.

How my coaching journey unfolded

I began coaching while an intern industrial psychologist at a South African transport company. Later, I worked as a registered psychologist for a bank where I was responsible for testing, assessing and developing people for management and leadership positions. For assessment, I followed up with feedback and coaching sessions with the individuals involved. In that way, I felt assured that they would accept the results and feel well-disposed towards behavioural adaptation.

Through the coaching assignments, I facilitated the processes that helped clients confront and manage their own stress factors. These stressors included low levels of self-esteem, a lack of balance between work and life, role confusion and interpersonal conflicts, nonperformance and even posttraumatic stress.

Almost by default, I learnt that the best application of my personal skills and characteristics was in a coaching process linked to focused assessment and development. It was clear to me that, when training is followed by coaching, much more transfer of learning takes place than when training is conducted in isolation. Learners have the time to engage with their new learning, in the presence of an aware coach who helps them think it through.

I reasoned that focused assessments allowed the assessed people to get their heads around their strengths and developmental needs. In this way those people received help from a coach who acted as a sounding board and thinking partner. The coach is also someone who understands that embracing such feedback requires courage, conviction and a positive approach.

My coaching journey has taken me around Africa, Europe, the United States of America and the United Kingdom. During this period, I have become increasingly confident that any successful facilitation of change in another's mind-set requires a highly trusting and one-on-one relationship between that person and a skilled coach who knows how to listen attentively. Of course, other coaching skills are essential too; however, in my mind, the art of good listening is paramount. The ability of the coach to accept the clients for who they are becomes crucial when their backgrounds differ from that of the coach, whether culturally, spiritually, socially and/or intellectually. Moreover, I found much delight in playing an instrumental role in helping others realise their potential, raise their own possibilities and make their own choices.

The coach's values: How do they emerge in the coaching?

Firstly, like any coach worth her salt, I believe that I should strive to leave clients in a much better place than where I found them. Given my background, I have come to respect people of all cultures, societies and religions however different they may be to my own – and however distant our value systems. Accordingly, I engage in coaching relationships with such clients where they, in turn, accept and respect where I come from.

Secondly, values are at the centre of my personal belief system, comprising respect, fairness and honesty. This set of values drives my thoughts and my behaviour and has become a key determinant of my coaching style.

Thirdly, I believe that contracting (formally or informally) is imperative, as parties tend to feel more comfortable when rights, responsibilities and commitments are reduced to writing. Thus goals, timelines and measurable outcomes are defined, enabling an objective evaluation of results. I prefer critical aspects such as handover and disengagement to be defined and agreed upfront – human nature typically finds a constructive coaching relationship painful to terminate.

Fourthly, I believe that my approach is to first seek to understand others and then to be understood. Part of the coaching process is to begin to understand the clients' values, beliefs, feelings and the systems in which they operate. This is the only way to unearth clients' views and constructs. The approach implies thorough open-ended questioning, with a keen focus on body language for additional clues to the meaning of the client's verbal message.

Both big and small improvements are important in coaching. People, however, are complex creatures and react differently when faced with a common situation. With some clients, big strides are possible; with others the coach needs to find satisfaction in facilitating incremental learning in small bites. Many coaches have come to appreciate that the small changes tend to endure longer than the big, bold and dramatic ones we sometimes see. I have come to appreciate the benefits of both approaches.

As I "mature" as a coach I am much more aware of the need to sense and balance the messages coming from both the conscious and the subconscious mind (objective and subjective) before judging or deciding. This is a personal practice that has stood me in good stead, especially during times of critical decision-making, and that I, through reflective practice, try to impart to those clients who are interested in ongoing personal growth. When becoming aware of a preconceived idea, usually a message from the subconscious mind, I use a cognitive behaviour form of self-coaching. In this way, I identify the activator to the negative thought and replace it with a more constructive one to facilitate an outcome that is positive and helpful to the client.

Another key focus as coach is to assist the clients to widen their circle of control as they decrease their areas of concern. This is achieved by increasing awareness of the client's own feelings, thoughts and intentions, as well as those of others who may be involved. Clients should be resourceful in exploring their own situations and creating options to deal with them. Often, all they need is a gentle push or pull in the right direction.

I believe that clients need to take responsibility for their own thoughts and actions, and commit themselves to either reinforce or change them. Unsolicited advice from the coach sometimes has negative repercussions later in the coaching process.

Client perceptions – the only reality

Any phenomenon may represent a suitable starting point for an investigation. My clients' perceptions serve as the essential beginning for meaningful conversations. With clients, a positive self-perception can grow in intensity, while negative self-esteem has the capacity to destroy most learning efforts. I have seen too that building someone's self-esteem is one of the most meaningful contributions a coach can make to clients achieving success in their careers, and in turn contributing to the success of their organisation.

The perceptions of my clients are therefore the only realities I work with. I try not to impose my own way of thinking or doing on my clients. Having taken the lead and noted a positive response, I attempt to blend into the background as the process unfolds. Consequently, the client feels in control of the outcomes of the session. Success, satisfaction and happiness are abstract constructs; for me the degree of client satisfaction is reflected by their newly formed perceptions, which lead to sustainable behaviour and attained goals.

Closer to home, on the subject of coaching in South Africa, authors Craig O'Flaherty and Janine Everson, both from the Centre for Coaching at the University of Cape Town's Graduate School of Business, report some fascinating findings on how the peoples of my country are informed by their "intricate social identities".[5] Their work reminds me that my clients' responses to the myriad expectations they face on a daily basis often involve the selection of an "appropriate identity" among many possible ones, which include but are not limited to (and are perhaps a mix of) "mother, daughter, wife, sister, sports fan, violinist, friend and colleague". Although this piece of writing focuses mainly on the benefits of using the Integral Model, the lesson I take from it is that your awareness of the social identity of your client is key to choosing the most appropriate approach to and model for coaching and to "owning it" (that is, it resonates with your perspectives and purpose for coaching).

Developing a signature presence

A key activity that executive managers perform to energise themselves and others involves the use of their voice, presence and influence. Those elements reflect the coach's **signature presence** and do so within ethical and moral boundaries. In my role as a professional coach, I act like a manager in the sense that I focus on the pursuit of organisational goals and the long-term growth of the client's business.

From the executive coach and author Mary Beth O'Neill I learnt about developing my personal signature presence as coach. I first had to reflect on **who I am**. It required me to hold up a mirror to myself – to test this passion that strives to bring the best of myself to all the roles I choose to play and those roles sometimes expected of me. Developing my own signature presence was a process. It involved developing a host of skills such as dealing with my own stress and anxieties and having the courage to speak out in conflict situations, yet it also involved my becoming invisible in coaching sessions.[6] I am therefore able to execute my role as professional coach in a way that is unique to me.

The core activity that great leaders perform is to use their voice, presence and power, ethically and within moral boundaries, to energise themselves and others. In the same way, I gravitated towards:

- finding my own authentic and unique voice
- making a difference through my signature presence
- using my power wisely

Once a shared concern has been established with the client and the contracting has been done, I act as partner with my client in a highly interactive coaching process. The **backbone** and **heart** approach advocated by O'Neill[7] comprises the two elements of backbone and heart. Bringing **backbone** into the coaching requires an inner strength to disagree with the client where necessary, while **heart** strives to continue the engagement with compassion, even in the face of conflict within the relationship. The two are highly interrelated elements that must, of necessity, work closely together.

Quite often, straddling the two elements of **heart** and **backbone** is like balancing delicately on a tightrope in a strong crosswind while moving on with the coaching process.

From an early stage in my coaching career I found satisfaction in watching the levels of client personal awareness move from being unconscious and static to becoming conscious and mobile – in various directions. Above all else, I wanted to make a meaningful contribution to South Africa, my home country, with its multitudes of citizens who needed help to develop their potential. I felt that I could achieve standards of excellence in the field of professional coaching. After all, I have developed a unique approach that combines team and one-on-one interactions with a systems approach to shared values.

The cumulative effect of my gradual yet deepening convictions strengthened my belief that I would find immense job satisfaction in the role of professional coach.

MY TEAM COACHING WORK

A substantial part of this book (chapters 4 to 8) is based on my coaching work at an engineering firm in Scandinavia, where I was commissioned in October 2004 to help with the development of a preferred organisational culture. A key requirement of the brief was that the new culture had to find agreement with all members of the executive team.

The company concerned wanted a structure for the automotive industry that would align the cultures of its six different business units into one. It emerged that key members of the executive team held the view that values are the essence of corporate identity and culture. That particular view encouraged me, as it resonated with earlier work that I had done. The popular philosophy in the company was that values underpin culture, and that what a company **does** (its **business focus**) is as critical as the **way** in which it pursues its business focus (its **values and cultural focus**).

In a nutshell, my function at the company was to devise and drive a coaching process that would find unanimous agreement on a preferred organisational culture within the executive team. Being well aware that agreement alone would never change a culture, we all resolved that the shift had to be guided by a set of personal and team indicators, which would eventually be used to confirm that the preferred culture was in place.

CONCLUSION

This chapter largely describes the personal values base that influenced my evolution as a professional coach. I have articulated my beliefs about signature presence and touched on the coaching work that helped me develop my own coaching approach. The next chapter discusses values, how they become shared in an organisation and the impact they may have on it. You can also read about the complexity of culture, with its many facets and the role it plays in business decisions.

Chapter 2

VALUES, ONCE AGREED AND SHARED, PROMOTE TEAM PERFORMANCE

A sneak-peek into this chapter ... We absolutely do have a say in the values we embrace. The attitudes we hold and the actions we take are personal choices. When we take a few quiet seconds to ponder our choices, we may find they produce heart-reaching and not just far-reaching effects.

INTRODUCTION

Chapter 1 explained the importance of coaching as a developmental tool to increase the levels of performance of individuals and teams by realising potential and tapping into underused strengths. In this chapter, I discuss human values and culture and their impact on the creation of a preferred way of **being** in organisations. Equally important is aligning cultural factors towards performance that is reinforced by appropriate reward systems for all stakeholders.

As I explained earlier, my primary aim when coaching is to increase levels of self-awareness regarding ownership by the client. I do this with a strong foundation that supports both personal and team goals. My personal coaching framework, which is discussed in the next chapter, promotes the alignment of individuals in an organisation with regard to how they think, feel and behave. Later, in chapter 5, the focus moves to a process that ensures alignment of teams of leaders and managers with a corporate culture guided by a set of corporate values. It is critical for business success that values are shared at all levels in the organisation.

HOW DO VALUES BECOME SHARED?

At this point it will be useful to understand the term **values**, which Steve Pavlina[8] sees as priorities that tell you how to spend your time, right here, right now. He says: "The main benefit of knowing your values is that you gain tremendous clarity and focus", and adds that this knowledge "facilitates consistency in decision-making and commitment to action". With regard to living personal values, Paul Hoffman[9] suggests that "leaders must wear them openly, constantly encouraging, mentoring, and coaching others to operate within the values-based and ethical standards the leader expresses".

We absolutely do have a say in the values we embrace. I also believe the attitudes we hold and the actions we take are personal choices. When we take a few quiet seconds to ponder our choices, we may find they produce heart-reaching and not just far-reaching effects.

How do we translate values into practice? As human beings we have the capacity to create abstract concepts to explain reality and to imagine a future reality different from the current one. We can also use abstract concepts such as values to guide our own behaviour towards a preferred future reality.[10] In the context of my work, the values of a group of people create a culture within that group that provides the framework within which to make decisions and take actions. Please allow me to call it a collective way of **being and doing**, which can evolve or can be consciously chosen. Similarly, organisations can make choices about values and a particular culture that would be instrumental in bringing about organisational renewal or culture change.

The seeds of change lie within us. We need to create the conditions necessary for the development of these seeds through "discussion with others which goes beyond our day-to-day work and deals with our deeper hopes and fears for our work, our organisations and our connections with others".[11] The author Frederic Hudson believes that these intimate conversations create the type of climate that offers a mutual support capable of transcending differences in values, beliefs and opinions.

The work of a trusted friend, Guy Charlton, reminds me that "at heart, every human being yearns to be treated with respect, to be involved, creative, have a sense of meaning in life, to feel good about what they do, to be part of a winning team and to have the chance to excel". On the subject of creating synergy between employees and organisations of choice, his advice is to "either **change** the leaders or change the **leaders**".[12]

CULTURE AND ITS ROLE IN BUSINESS DECISIONS

Culture is a complex topic with many facets, such as symbols, language, ideologies, rituals, myths and patterns of behaviour. I want to focus on human value and belief systems, and the impact they have on the creation and reinforcement of organisational behaviour. We have come to understand that culture is created and sustained by human beings – their values, beliefs, needs, expectations, emotional intelligence and especially their behaviours. Tony Manning[13] sees change in behaviour, rather than change in thinking, as the priority when he suggests that culture is as much a cause as a consequence of behaviour. For me, this is a profound statement, since it moves an individual from victim to master of his or her own behaviour, and in my book it places the responsibility for the facilitation of a common culture in the hands of business leaders.

Richard S Gallagher[14] supports this notion when he says that culture is ultimately determined by how we respond to business decisions, since these are governed by our core values. Richard Bellingham[15] agrees that values act as a benchmark or barometer against which certain business decisions may be checked.

Marc Kahn[16] refers to the work of Schein, who offered a functional perspective of the evolutionary process, explaining that in order for an organisation to survive the following two fundamental issues need to be resolved:

- the capacity of the group to work together in a significantly cohesive and coordinated way to sustain itself into the future. He refers to this capability as **internal integration**.
- the challenge of surviving into the future by adapting to the external environment, which he terms a process of **external adaptation**.

Quoting the organisational culture expert Majken Schultz, Kahn concludes on the matter of culture: "The internal integration of culture serves as 'consensus-creating glue' which, in turn, creates cohesion in the group." From the external point of view, "culture acts to adapt the group to the demands of a changing and complex external environment world".[17]

Corporate values act as the operating philosophies or principles that guide an organisation's internal conduct, as well as its relationship with customers, partners and shareholders. "Values are based upon our belief systems about what is desirable for the long-term growth of the corporation, rather than about what is right or wrong".[18] Corporate values become shared when they are adopted and lived out by all the employees in an organisation.

Shared values lead to a preferred way of doing and being which ultimately results in a discernible change in culture. Culture is also what the employees perceive and how this perception creates a pattern of behaviour in the workplace.[19] It follows that a preferred organisational culture may be viewed as a future state, purposefully deliberated by the leaders and key stakeholders. That future state will indicate how things must be done in the organisation from an agreed date.

The assertion that shared values are integral to instilling a preferred organisational culture has been recently supported by a growing number of experts around the world.

The sharing of core values and beliefs through coaching seems to be a viable strategy through which to achieve the transition from concept to practice. That may be easier said than done. The truth about walking the talk, as put by Carolyn Taylor[20], is that "you can't fake it!" Taylor adds that it is about who you are, the values you endorse as a leader and the embodiment of the values you pass down to the next level of managers to ensure alignment in behaviour.

VALUE CREATION FACILITATES LONG-TERM GAINS THROUGH SHARED LEADERSHIP PRACTICE

Personal experience in corporate business relating to strategy and culture has convinced me that at times too much focus is placed on short-term gains, which are achieved at the expense of long-term growth. In my opinion, the gradual creation of value is a better option than engaging in any relentless pursuit of short-term gains. Value creation needs introspection regarding the key values and beliefs of the organisation's leaders. They should live and even breathe the selected values in their day-to-day interactions with stakeholders.

Organisational culture experts Hopkins, Hopkins and Mallette[21] underscore my own belief when they state that leaders tend to "overlook corporate culture as a source of competitive advantage for the organisation" and undervalue the central role it plays in the organisation's ability to create and sustain competitive advantage. The authors reason that corporate culture influences business conduct in the sense that it drives all behaviour towards customers, both internally and externally.

Values become shared when repeatedly reinforced, especially by the leader and the managers in the organisation.

Mary C Gentile[22] teaches us to speak our mind when we know that we are right. She promotes the conscious development **script** that managers and leaders should use when they are faced with value-based challenges in the organisation. This script is the collective, informed and consciously chosen responses of the team to value-based challenges. Instead of rationalising decisions in the light of what others are doing, the script comes from a place of competence and conviction where collective responsibility is used.

Shared tactics are some of the indicators that Randy Pennington[23] sees as representative of the organisation's culture. He makes a case for leaders to choose an organisational culture that engages all stakeholders in the company's mission. Pennington suggests that the resulting benefits revolve around effective partnerships and teams, and a focus on what is good and not on what comes easily. He relates success stories of companies such as Toyota and Nordstrom, where carefully researched organisational cultures won the hearts, minds and loyalty of employees and customers.

How is it then that shared organisational values sustain performance and competitiveness? Well, my first experience of working with an engineering team where I assisted with alignment taught me that shared values steer behaviour into new directions which have the potential to create a new organisational culture (a collective way of doing and being). A strong culture recognises and reinforces certain behaviours in similar ways to **conditioning**, where people tend to show the behaviours that are rewarded positively, but shy away from those behaviours that result in censure.

Most individuals welcome some form of recognition. When made to feel good about their behaviour, they tend to repeat this behaviour and in so doing, help to reinforce the resulting culture. This was the case with one of the leadership teams I was privileged to work with. They took the initiative of incorporating their goals into their business scorecard (BSC), for a different way of leading. Once they had linked goal achievement to recognition and reward, they soon regarded the need to change their way of doing things in a more serious light. Goal-directed actions followed, bringing improved work performance and financial results.

Richard Bellingham[24] suggests that shared values facilitate a process whereby individuals feel they can contribute to the vision of the organisation. He sees shared values as a benchmark against which corporate decisions may be evaluated. Bellingham also believes that values establish purpose and inform strategy. My experience had already taught me that people readily take part in any exercise where values are being shared. And so my response to Bellingham is that it is all well and good to say that shared values have to be established. However, the biggest single challenge is the translation of values into behaviour in line with organisational goals. In other words, **walking the talk for real**, and in such a way that other stakeholders experience the values on the corporate wall as authentic, is to my mind the key factor in making values become practical in organisations.

As most companies are confronted with the need to improve competitiveness, a natural response is a stronger focus on customer service, linked to incentives aimed at motivating staff to display behaviour that would promote this ideal. My own hypothesis is that companies have a better chance of being customer-oriented when led by someone who sees the economic sense in being customer-focused and treating customers exceptionally well. Cultures are then maintained through the messages that are sent, often by leaders, showing what **good** looks like, referring to behaviours that are accepted and expected.

Roger Harrison[25] explains that culture is the key to understanding service when he says: "The service offered by the organisation, both internally and to its customers, reflects that combination of values, preoccupations, social structure, norms and mores which we call organisational culture." He also agrees that **walking the talk** is what matters most. To simply believe that customers need to be seen as kings without doing anything about it is not good enough. Lip service alone won't get the job done. "Leadership is not about our intent, but all about our effect on others", say Ungerer, Herholdt and Le Roux[26].

THE VALUE QUESTIONS

The value questions emerging here could lead to meaningful answers for corporate leaders:

- What values would we feel proud to see exercised in the business through leadership style?
- How would we achieve that?
- Which values will instil the type of organisational culture we want in the business?
- What strategy would we use to ensure that people's beliefs and values are aligned with the ways we should treat associates, peers and customers, both internally and externally?
- What process should we follow to ensure that these values become shared?

For these questions to translate into a successful and meaningful leadership legacy, agreement must be reached by all leaders in the organisation about the behaviours that will underpin the chosen core values for open and willing support. When working with teams that wish to achieve alignment with regard to their values, the coach needs to create a space that allows for total honesty and that protects those who allow themselves to be vulnerable. These spaces facilitate a willingness and courage to look reflectively in the mirror with humility, yet without reproach.

THE LEADERSHIP ALIGNMENT CHALLENGE

During my education in coaching and the subsequent practising of coaching with leaders and their teams, my take on the leadership alignment challenge is that alignment can be achieved by implementing five key steps:

- Decide what the preferred culture should look like.
- Compare it to the current culture.
- Note the gap between the ideal preferred culture and the current reality.
- Determine the leadership and management practices that would best facilitate the mobilisation of the stakeholders towards the preferred culture.
- Practise these and make them part of the everyday leadership approach while integrating them into measurement practice to ensure sustainability.

THE IMPORTANCE OF CULTURAL ALIGNMENT

Leaders with insight into the link between organisational culture and performance understand the need to align all stakeholders to create wealth, to sustain the future of the organisation and to provide meaning and purpose for all involved. Alignment brings synergy. Other elements such as accord and harmony among business units or departments greatly enhance the identification of shared goals and the constructive use of **together time**.

My team-coaching clients report that being aligned makes for strong interpersonal relationships and rewarding behaviour agreed by the team. They claim that this, in turn, facilitates the very essence of their team culture because it reinforces behaviours agreed by the team. The conclusion I most certainly arrive at after having studied a variety of teams in various countries is this: If organisations are to achieve and sustain a competitive advantage in the marketplace, the process of cultural alignment must begin with the leaders of key business units and then be cascaded downward in a controlled sequence.

In what he calls a guidebook for "teamlanders" (people who spend most of their waking hours in teams and/or rely on and/or connect with and work through teams), Peter Hawkins addresses some key issues relating to the creation, enablement and alignment of teams.[27] The significance to me of his teaching is the clear message that we need to co-create new thinking that energises, connects and refocuses our collective energy towards the continual regeneration of not just our teams but also those we purport to empower. In her doctoral thesis, Louise van Rhyn shared the belief that successful practitioners of organisational change have a way to harness the new sense that is being made through dialogue, as these practitioners have realised that the Process of Culture (formation, shift, renewal or reinforcment) happens through organised processes of interaction in organisations.[28] Van Rhyn's exceptional leadership in creating partnerships between business leaders and school principals is widely known, and has been captured in the book *Partners for Possibility*.[29]

How do we as coaches influence the dialogue? This is the question that comes up for me. Schein proposes that leaders need to realise when their imposed values and perceptions (the culture they created) need to be changed or adapted. Also, leaders must show a willingness to step away from their current ways and consider more appropriate ways of thinking and doing.[30]

Dr Morne Mostert[31] talks about the **company way** as unwritten rules that "sculpt and perpetuate a culture that governs the behaviour of leaders and subsequently, the behaviour of their staff". He suggests that every possible opportunity for people to learn is an opportunity to evolve – only if the organisation allows for divergence of thinking and for new knowledge to enter the system.

Careful measurement allows organisations to compare results for different business units, and also helps them to gain insight into the relationship between work culture and organisational performance. A strong culture that facilitates future business strategy and sustained financial performance needs leaders and managers to raise the bar in terms of performance standards.[32] In contrast, one of the most frequent causes of failed organisational interventions is neglecting the role played by the distinctive organisational culture in the achievement of strategic objectives.[33]

Kaplan and Norton[34] believe that Hall of Fame organisations, meaning those companies that have demonstrated successful implementation of their strategies using a performance management system based on the BSC, are much better at aligning their corporate, business unit and support unit strategies, which indicates that alignment produces dramatic benefits. My training in the use of the BSC mainly for purposes of measuring the success of strategy implementation, and my personal reflection, tell me that any company that takes its culture seriously will include both strategic (**what to achieve**) goals and cultural (**how to achieve it**) goals on one and the same scorecard.

ALIGNING SUBCULTURES AND THEIR VALUES

In a study related to this topic, Hopkins et al[35] found that the more employees are committed to key organisational values, the stronger the organisation's corporate culture. Their results show that employees in organisations with strong corporate cultures are more committed to the organisation's values than employees in organisations with weak corporate cultures.

THE IMPACT OF SUBCULTURES

Subcultures are a reality in all organisations; they may be based on membership of various groups, such as departments, work groups and teams, and on geographical areas. Differences in work orientation, with respect to targets, client groups, interrelationships, hierarchy and work methods, promote the forming of distinct and even opposing values within these subcultures. The more distinctive the value system of the subculture, the stronger the potential for misalignment seems to be. This strengthens my belief that subcultures must be deliberately aligned if organisations are to achieve and sustain a competitive advantage in the marketplace, maintain their customer base, require less marketing activity and lower sales-related expenditure.

CONCLUSION

An agreed preferred culture becomes entrenched when people respond to appropriate cues and become aligned with organisational values. In such organisations, strongly aligned subcultures create synergy between work components, resulting in easier work functioning with less bureaucracy. By contrast, a weak organisational culture with strong yet misaligned subcultures demands greater levels of effort and direction by managers.

An organisation with a strong organisational culture and shared values finds easier acceptance by employees and outside stakeholders. The culture is easier to **live** when led by the leaders. Consequently, strong cultures have increased employee alignment with the organisation's vision, mission and goals. Loyalty and motivation are found in larger measures throughout the organisation. There is also greater team cohesion between the various work units and greater levels of efficiency, effectiveness and long-term growth.

In chapter 3, I share the multiple perspectives that inform my coaching (including theories, practices and my personal experience, values and beliefs); I also set out my purpose for coaching and how it has evolved. I introduce the framework and model I use in my coaching, particularly in the one-on-one sessions with clients.

Chapter 3

HOW ALL THAT WE LEARN, EXPERIENCE AND BELIEVE SHAPES OUR COACHING APPROACH

The message that I want to convey in this chapter is that everything we are, know, believe and have experienced in life is relevant to our coaching practices. Learning to become a professional coach allows us to revisit our experiences, values, beliefs and worldviews quite critically as we become mindful of the harm that we can do to our clients if we are not aware of our own "stuff". Furthermore, making peace with who we are, what we bring to a client relationship, what we don't bring and how we do so, shows care and consideration for our clients; one of the most fundamental rules of coaching is "do no harm".

INTRODUCTION

I firmly believe that personal values, leadership values and team values can all be embraced consciously, becoming tools that allow one to choose new behaviours (thinking, doing, speaking and being), helping to bring meaning and value to one's life. However, there needs to be alignment among the values that an individual declares, whether they are personal or professional, and those values representing his or her peer group or team. I believe that it is this alignment with self (the self in various situations) that has become the essence of my purpose for coaching.

After writing my first version of this chapter, I had to do some serious reflection on "how it would come across". My intention with this chapter is to inspire those of you who are on a journey to discover your own coaching frameworks and models. The only way I can do this is to take you through my own journey. It took a reread of the last chapter of *The Complete Handbook of Coaching* to remind me of the value of having our frameworks and approaches underpinned by theories and practices that resonate with us. This will help to ensure that the services we offer are authentic and believable.[36]

So, with this chapter, I introduce the personal perspectives, purpose and process that underpin my work. I explain how these came about and how they guide my conduct as coach. In short, a coaching model is a collective collage on which you draw continuously; it is made up of everything that informs you, how you coach and all that you leave behind with your client. The model I present in this chapter is mainly aimed at one-on-one coaching, whereas the process I cover in later chapters was designed to offer a combined coaching approach (team coaching followed by one-on-one coaching as a double-loop learning process). Please appreciate that, as with all coaches, this model is still evolving and will always be!

In this chapter, I also reflect on my learning from the disciplines of training, organisational development and assessment of potential. The message that I want to bring home to those readers who are considering becoming coaches or who are currently being educated in professional coaching is that all that you are and know and have experienced inform your coaching. Isn't that just awesome! The very fact that you are unique in what makes up your offering as coach ensures that you will find your own special niche in the coaching world. There is no other coach quite like you in this world and there are clients out there who need your special offering! At the end of this chapter, you should have a better appreciation of the concept of shared values, particularly in relation to leadership teams that are committed to aligning thoughts and behaviours towards agreed corporate goals.

Theoretically, most initiatives aimed at cultural change have the potential to become positive and even enjoyable experiences for the parties involved. In practice, however, change can become anything but pleasant, even when consistent with agreed desires. Dissonance, which is a state of internal discord, is created when people have to move away from established norms and do things differently. That is, there is conflict between what decision-makers know and believe, and what has to be done. As a result, doubt often arises about choices made.[37]

The concept I embraced to reduce uncertainty was to promote the road to renewal as a creative, fun and worthwhile journey. Why "renewal" and not change? I found that the mental picture that the word "change" conjured up is one of loss rather than gain.

The intervention constitutes the plan of getting from the **now** to the **future** state or the new vision. And so it made sense for me to visualise the end result of every change initiative before examining the current situation in any detail. Getting from **here** to **there** is not as painless as it may sound.

THE PROCESS OF CULTURAL RENEWAL

Transformation processes bring about changes of all kinds. Some of the things that need to be changed may be entrenched practices cherished by people in the organisation. Hence, giving them up can lead to what most people see as a loss, which detracts from what I call **me action**. Put simply, changing practices (thoughts and behaviour) involves examining the way things are done in the organisation and then collectively agreeing on the answers to these questions:

- Which are the things that are good and should be retained and strengthened?
- Which are the practices that should go?
- Which are the new practices that should be embraced?

Executive coach Janice Steed[38] summarises it well when she says that coaching can help us access and build the positive resources already present within individuals and organisations, encouraging people to find their own solutions and generating day-to-day conversations. Enhancing what is already being done well can have a transformative effect on individual and collective performance and will generate impact far beyond the organisation itself.

Soon after I started coaching teams, I realised that my clients and I would often come from very different cultures and disciplines, a situation that presented challenges with communication and interpretation. Our worldviews (the culmination of our upbringing, learning and experiences) might be different too. As I gained experience in coaching teams and as I reflected on this, I realised that diversity was not a stumbling block but a challenge. The challenge for me as a coach was to ensure that everyone who was part of the team felt welcome, respected and valued. Some later reflections revealed that the real challenge was to get all team members to treat each other with respect and especially to value each member and include everyone in the discussion. Through all of this, I had to stay mindful of how I was different to my clients (in terms of beliefs, worldview, experiences and the like) in order to keep them in high regard and treat them with respect on this journey of discovery together as coach and clients.

SHARED CONCERNS

Early on in my coaching journey, I learnt that one could hardly call a conversation "coaching" if a **shared concern did not exist between coach and client** – a powerful construct I learnt from David Lane's book *The Impossible Child*.[39] Lane's book provided the foundation of the special client-coach relationship I needed for the Swedish project to succeed.

A shared concern develops once the coach and the client begin to examine the areas of concern when faced with a situation or challenge, especially where differing viewpoints are held. Once the core challenges have been defined, it becomes possible to identify aspects that can be readily shared by both parties, thus forming a basis for focused exploration.

Simply stated, a shared concern reflects the place reached by client and coach where both become conscious of and find agreement on any or all of the following:

- an opportunity to be grasped
- a mind-set to be changed
- a performance goal to be reached

In my view, coach and clients truly engage in coaching only when they have reached this place of shared concern and not before. This is why it is crucial for me to hear the client's complete story before being able to do two things:

- Distil the real need for coaching.
- Develop any meaningful and relevant focus for the coaching engagement.

I knew that my need to formalise the contracting part of the coaching relationship could give rise to some uncertainty with my Swedish clients, and in this contracting lay the source of some of the dissonance or internal conflict I felt. Let me explain.

CONTRACTING

What is contracting? Well, it is the process of formalising any procedure or agreement. However, contracting goes far beyond simply reducing matters to writing. It is really a critical engagement that begins at first contact with the client to be coached and it is arguably the most important part of the overall coaching process. Coaching is multi-pronged, beginning with getting accepted by the client and leading, in its final stage, to the client realising that he or she too could be part of the problem.

Does a handshake indicate mutual consent?

One of the basic beliefs of many a culture is that **a handshake is generally good enough** and therefore it is not necessary to formalise every single agreement. This is not the way I have learnt to do things though, and I am keenly aware that my need to contract properly needs to be communicated with lots of emotional intelligence lest my clients think that I do not trust them. So there is potential for conflict if I do not take the client's responsibilities upon my shoulders as my own.

When I function as an outsider coach, the organisation's problems are not really mine. I therefore take the bull by the horns and then hand the problems right back to the organisation. This means that in any professional coaching relationship there are "those delicate times that call for bold initiative" from the coach while simultaneously following the client's lead.[40]

I have experienced the roles of consultant and coach very differently in terms of approach. In a consultative role, it is ethically acceptable to provide clear advice and direction. However, in a coaching relationship it is better to allow clients to find their own way and generate their own options and solutions. Leading on from this, I found it useful to clarify my new role in every session – for my own sake, as well as that of the client.

We learn as we coach and our learning continually shapes our approach to and model of coaching and our increased efficiency and professionalism as coaches. The most precious part is the ongoing learning, yet it is also the most frustrating part for "coaches in training". How can we consistently be and do the same if our insight into ourselves, our clients and our processes is shaped daily by our interaction with different clients?

My coaching is greatly informed by the **conscious competence theory**, since it helps me to better understand the coaching process and, in particular, how new skills, behaviours and techniques may be learnt. The matrix in table 3.1 shows how this theory plays out when learning a skill. When you read through it, please remember that coaching facilitates learning, not only of skills but also of mind-sets, behaviours and a whole lot more. Later in this book, I show you how I returned to this theory to make sense of a team-coaching process that I had developed.

An earlier description of the modern-day conscious competence model is featured in the article *Teaching for Learning* by Martin M Broadwell, dated 20 February 1969[41], in *The Gospel Guardian*, an American Christian periodical published from the 1950s to 1970s, for those of you who find this theory meaningful.

Initially described as "Four Stages for Learning Any New Skill", the **conscious competence theory** was developed by Noel Burch of Gordon Training International in the 1970s[42]. It has since been attributed to Abraham Maslow, although the model does not appear in his major works.

Table 3.1: Four stages of the conscious competence theory

	Competence	Incompetence
Conscious	**Stage 3: conscious competence** • The person achieves "conscious competence" in a skill when he or she can perform it reliably at will. • The person will need to concentrate and think in order to perform the skill. • The person can perform the skill without assistance. • The person will not reliably perform the skill unless thinking about it – the skill is not yet "second nature" or "automatic". • The person should be able to demonstrate the skill to another, but is unlikely to be able to teach it well to another person. • The person should ideally continue to practise the new skill, and if appropriate commit to becoming "unconsciously competent" at the new skill. • Practise is the most effective way to move from stage 3 to stage 4.	**Stage 2: conscious incompetence** • The person becomes aware of the existence and relevance of the skill. • The person is therefore also aware of his or her deficiency in this area, ideally by attempting to use the skill. • The person realises that by improving his or her skill or ability in this area, he or she will become more effective. • Ideally, the person has a measure of the extent of his or her deficiency in the relevant skill, and a measure of what level of skill is required for his or her own competence. • The person ideally makes a commitment to learn and practise the new skill, and to move to the "conscious competence" stage.
Unconscious	**Stage 4: unconscious competence** • The skill becomes so practised that it enters the unconscious parts of the brain – it becomes "second nature". • Common examples are driving, sports activities, typing, manual dexterity tasks, listening and communicating. • It becomes possible to perform certain skills while doing something else, for example, knitting while reading a book. • The person might now be able to teach others the skill concerned, although after some time of being unconsciously competent the person might actually have difficulty in explaining exactly how he or she does it – the skill has become largely instinctual. • This arguably gives rise to the need for long-standing unconscious competence to be checked periodically against new standards.	**Stage 1: unconscious incompetence** • The person is not aware of the existence or relevance of the skill area. • The person is not aware that he or she has a particular deficiency in the area concerned. • The person might deny the relevance or usefulness of the new skill. • The person must become conscious of his or her incompetence before the development of the new skill or learning can begin. • The aim of the trainee or learner and the trainer or teacher is to move the person into the "conscious competence" stage by demonstrating the skill or ability and the benefit that it will bring to the person's effectiveness.

Source: www.businessballs.com/consciouscompetencelearningmodel.htm[43]

MY JOURNEY THROUGH THE CORPORATE WORLD

My journey through the corporate world, and in particular my role as an industrial psychologist, stimulated the development of my own coaching model with cognitive behavioural therapy as its foundation and spiritual awareness as an essential outcome.

I have spent time in the corporate environment during three stages in my career: firstly while carving my own niche as a trainer, secondly as a facilitator and thirdly as a counsellor or coach in private practice. Playing these roles brought challenges and personal growth in a coaching capacity as my focus shifted from one industry to another and across geographical and cultural boundaries.

Assessment centres

My experience in assessment centres sensitised me to the individualistic focus of most assessment products and processes. My exposure to assessments started with the South African Transport Services (now Transnet), and continued later in the banking sector. The focus then was on evaluating people and their performance against defined norms. Little attention was paid to how well (or how poorly) the person fitted into current or prospective work teams. There was little interest, too, in noting whether team members shared the same values, work approaches or perceptions of what makes for good performance.

It was during this period that I was introduced to self-assessment centres. The method empowered people to take some responsibility for their own assessment and provided structured tools and techniques, with support from an assessor who played a coaching role rather than an expert feedback role.

The approach was applied to natural work teams, with the result that fellow team members were much more informed about one another's strengths and developmental needs. They actively sought opportunities for closer working relationships and developed insight into the perceptions, norms, values and backgrounds of their team members. The induced interaction produced teams that remained close-knit, even after leaving the relative safety of the development centre for the real working environment.

Cohesive work teams

My experience with alignment within teams gave me satisfaction and the feeling of having made a contribution to the management development drive. As a response, in all my later participation in this line of work, I have included my clients in the process of discovering the skills, attributes and behaviours that facilitated success for them. I downplayed those elements that had caused underperformance, hindered interpersonal relationships and caused team members to question the meaning of their own lives and the contribution they made to society.

In that same period I made an interesting observation in the international organisation to which I was contracted. The company employed people from a wide variety of cultures. It thus became easy to note a significantly lower level of conflict among team members who came from similar cultural backgrounds compared to teams with members from a diversity of cultures. This realisation later assumed great importance in restructuring projects such as that of Viking Enterprises, which had set out to integrate its six independent business units into one cohesive entity.

The subsequent reorganisation of the work teams introduced a new combination based on skill and also on cultural grounds. That single change brought about a noticeable improvement in teamwork and, ultimately, client service.

Coaching and the transfer of skills

Whenever I contracted with clients as a facilitator of learning, I followed up on the training sessions with either small-group conversations or one-on-one conversations to ensure that learning was transferred to the workplace, even though that was not actually a specific function of mine. It just seemed the right thing to do. Little did I know that this type of conversation would later fall under the banner of **coaching**. I realised that the most rewarding dialogues for me were those that happened after a training or facilitation session where my role had been that of coach.

I felt excited by my self-assigned role of ensuring the successful transfer of new skills. My high levels of self-motivation continued after I had conducted training that was followed by coaching interventions to help integrate new concepts, behaviours and practices within teams or individuals. The internal drive was a natural expression of my own philosophy of learning. It emerged as an autonomous process at first. Later, I took active steps to entrench the behaviour within my coaching practices. Today, it forms part of my teaching in coaching.

My personal coaching model

Using small, progressive steps, I developed my own personal coaching model after adopting and amending the basic framework of David Lane with its phases of inputs, transformation and outputs[44].

My coaching model initially developed as part of my doctorate in coaching and has seen no fewer than 20 iterations to date. Essentially, the model comprises five phases of client interaction, mainly consisting of (but not limited to) one-on-one conversations. What follows is a short description of the five phases that constitute my personal coaching model. Please appreciate that each phase may need a number of sessions.

Phase 1: Exploring a partnership

Upon meeting clients who show interest in a coaching relationship, I always appreciate at least one or two extended sessions during which I invite them to tell me about themselves – what excites them, what gets them down – and to hear about the significant others in their lives. I also ask what is the single most important quest they aspire to at the time, perhaps an opportunity they want to seize.

During this phase I also share with them who I am in terms of what is relevant to a coaching relationship. Important to me is how they perceive their context, the responsibility to make a difference, changes and shifts, their points of reference, worldviews and, in particular, the lenses through which they look at their roles, place and purpose in their world. This phase progresses often, yet not always, to a point where I explore if the clients really want to work with me. They then make the choice, after which we agree, in general terms, on the preferred outcomes required from the coaching.

Of particular importance during this phase is to share our views on coaching. The potential client may or may not have been exposed to coaching. I respectfully probe the clients' knowledge of coaching and their particular need for coaching. Then I proceed to share my personal coaching approach with them and to explain whether or not I think that I am the most appropriate person to enter into a coaching relationship with them. In instances where the individual wants life coaching, I prefer to refer him or her to someone who does life coaching. This has to be a person I trust implicitly and whom I would personally consider for life coaching. If I suspect that the individual should rather receive counselling or therapy, I take care to explain the difference between coaching and counselling, and again offer some good references. Should we decide that we want to enter into a coaching relationship, we proceed to discuss how our personal values will find effect in our coaching and how confidentiality will be practised.

The key outcomes of this session are laying the foundation for a coaching relationship between client and coach, defining my role as coach and establishing my signature presence. Mary Beth O'Neil describes signature presence as "bringing yourself when you coach – your values, passion, creativity, emotion, and discerning judgement – to any given moment with a client"[45]. At this early point, the client is either **unconsciously incompetent** or **consciously incompetent**, depending on the sense of awareness of what is going on in his or her life, work, body and soul, and/or in relating to others.

What informs my approach during this session is an acute awareness of the complexity of people, the systems and processes of which they form a part, and the multitude of expectations that they and others have of them. My background as an industrial psychologist, consultant and trainer emerges and, of course, so does all the learning and experience that I have gained from the various schools of psychology and coaching that I have been exposed to. More importantly perhaps, my approach to coaching is also impacted by my love for work-based, action-orientated learning and my strong underpinning of Cognitive Behavioural Coaching, leadership and organisational theories and all of the intelligence models (emotional, relational, spiritual and natural).

Phase 2: Forming a pact

Professionally, I received my initial training in the era of quality circles and outcomes-based education. Much focus was placed on a total appreciation of the client and the **problem** presented. No effort was too big to adjust the service offering – **taking time to thank the client for sharing and asking what more could be done to meet any other related expectations.** This approach requires a strong sense of ownership of situations that arise, supported by a reasonable attempt to understand what the client is going through.

Rapport is of the essence during this stage. Previously explored areas of required growth (Phase 1) are reviewed, refined and reduced to a few realistic and meaningful objectives. Where these involve behavioural shifts, test hypotheses are created to capture the mind-set, words and/or feelings of clients when their challenges (both positive and developmental) are fully conquered.

The purpose of this stage is mainly to move the clients to a stage of conscious incompetence (knowing what they still have to learn) if they were not at this level of awareness during Phase 1. After this phase I am fully aware of the challenges that the client is already facing, and we have a shared concern. We are also fully committed to the work needed to address the situation or capture any worthwhile opportunity that presents itself. We have formed a pact. A definite output of this stage is reaching a proper contract around the mechanics, the dynamics and the ethical boundaries that will govern our coaching conversations.

Phase 3: Coaching with zest

During this stage of coaching, I carefully choose an approach that takes into account my client's need for support, intentions, wants, needs and abilities. Should the client wish to work on behaviour, my approach will be cognitively behavioural. If the situation needs to be performance-driven, I may explore the use of a performance-orientated model. When it comes to issues of faith, values and beliefs, my best offering is that of personal construct psychology with a healthy appreciation of the major influence that both coach and client relationships and spiritual intelligence has on the process. In later chapters I share the approach I use when coaching teams need and seek alignment.

Reflection on learning becomes an essential element of any approach that I elect to use and that I share with my client. Reflections in the moment are done continuously during sessions. I motivate and stimulate my clients to reflect after sessions, during periods back at work and again prior to the next session. The recording of reflections is key to the success of my coaching style and offering. Through these records, we make sense of what thoughts, habits and deep-seated beliefs have to be revisited, unlearnt, renewed and embraced. Together, we ensure that we complete the learning cycle, which essentially brings about sustainable adaptation, shift or renewal.

This stage of the coaching model entails a series of coaching sessions in which clients progress towards their preferred state of being, thinking and doing, while I keep the scaffold in place so that clients are safely **held** while reconstructing what is viable, relevant and meaningful to them.

OTHER MODALITIES OF VALUE

Other modalities that I have learnt from and that inform my coaching model during this phase include neuro-linguistic programming (NLP), force field analysis, De Bono's six thinking hats, questioning frameworks and mindfulness.

Neuro-linguistic programming

The field of NLP has taught me to build and keep up my rapport with the client. NLP explores the relationships between how we think (neuro-), how we communicate (linguistic) and our patterns of behaviour and emotions[46]. NLP training helps me to build rapport by becoming more aware of the physical presence and patterns of the client so that matching or mirroring states can be adopted.

Through many years of practice, I've learnt more from what people are not saying than from what they do say. For this reason, I meet my clients face to face for at least the first phase before I can coach them through the other media at my disposal. During this upfront and personal time with them, I make sense of their communicative trends and patterns, their voice modulations, how they express their emotions or how they choose not to, and I also note a myriad other physical clues that they provide during the interaction.

Through exposure to customer service training, I have learnt somewhere that the acronym GREAT reflects a set of guidelines for increased customer service. GREAT stands for **G**reeting, **R**especting, **E**valuating client needs, **A**djusting your offering and **T**hanking the customer for using you. I try to ensure that I apply all five of these service principles in all my sessions, as they help me to stay humble, curious and helpful.

Force field analysis

I often find myself sharing the useful technique of force field analysis with my clients. This is a decision-making technique which helps me as coach establish boundaries for myself and also for others. It guides my thinking and actions in a particular situation. Within boundaries lies the freedom to choose, decide and act.

Force field analysis was developed by Kurt Lewin[47] and it is widely used to inform decision-making, particularly in planning and implementing change management programmes in organisations. It is a powerful method of gaining a comprehensive overview of the different forces acting on a potential organisational change issue, and assessing their sources and strengths.

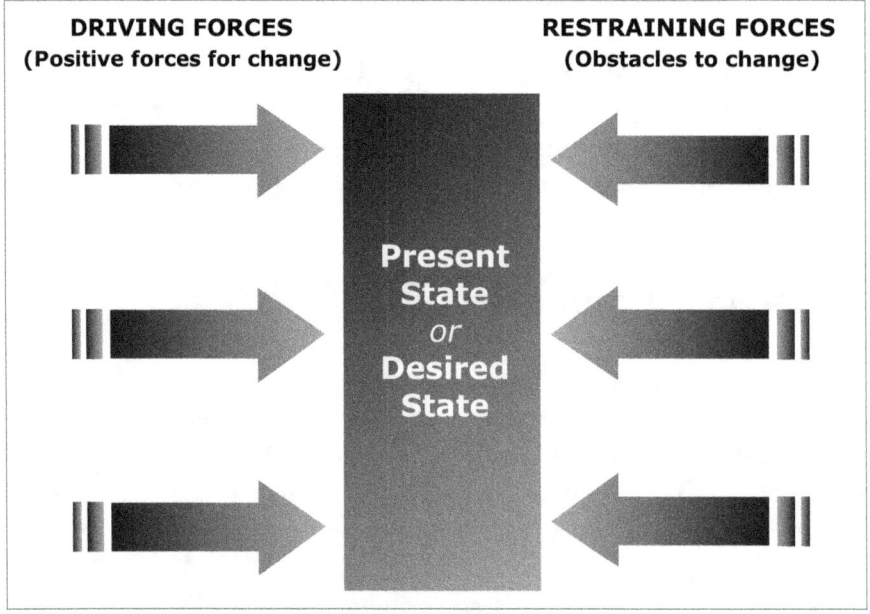

Source: Kurt Lewin at www.change-management-coach.com[48]
Figure 3.1: Basic force field analysis

The essence of Kurt Lewin's theory is that any issue is held in balance by the interaction of two major forces. The status quo is therefore kept in place by driving and resisting forces. Lewin calls this a social equilibrium. Used in the human sciences, it can distinguish factors within a certain context that will pull stakeholders towards the preferred or desired state, and forces that will push stakeholders away from the preferred or desired state. Here are examples of desired states:

- agreements between two parties, for instance on salary increases
- agreements between buyers and suppliers regarding the price to be paid for goods or services
- a preferred state or future state in an organisation, such as an organisational culture

In all the above examples, there will be those who oppose the preferred or desired state and those who welcome it. Both parties will come up with reasons why they do or do not want the preferred state to become a reality. When the facilitator knows the factors for and against a preferred outcome or state, it is easier to guide the discussion or negotiations. In doing so, any shift in forces will unsettle the equilibrium and a new equilibrium will be established.

In the same way, team coaches can use this technique to facilitate agreement about a preferred state within the team. To me, there is a difference between team facilitation and team coaching. I explain this in chapter 11.

When a team coach has been briefed to facilitate the team towards a specific outcome, the coach has clearer intentions about the outcome and may have a more leading and even directional approach. When the team coach has been briefed to ensure that a viable and relevant team agreement is sought, I believe that it calls for a coaching approach that is nondirectional and nonintentional.

Ingie Hovland's *Successful communication: A toolkit for researchers and civil society organisations*[49] provides more information on this topic.

The six thinking hats

When working with teams who experience dissonance, misalignment and/or conflict, I find the six thinking hats of Edward de Bono to be a relevant and useful technique. Although I am not a certified user of this technique, I have made a proper study of it and have tried it out in teams, explaining that it was experiential and that I was not a fundi.

When used during the coaching of teams, the various hats guide the team towards collective thinking about a situation, challenge or opportunity. In a subtle way, one can assist the team members to redirect their thinking processes as well as their interaction in the session by wearing the various hats at appropriate times. For example, when a certain issue has been known to raise negativity and extreme emotions, one could consider wearing the red and black hats first so that, with these out of the way, more positivity and creativity can be tapped into. The six hats are shown in figure 3.2.

Source: De Bono, 1999[50]

Figure 3.2: *The six thinking hats of Edward de Bono*

Questioning frameworks

Over the years, I have studied, used and taught many and varied questioning frameworks. As **I become a more seasoned** coach, I am mindful that these questions emerge not because I am clever, but because I have used them so often. I have also learnt that they have the potential to bring to the coaching experience a high level of **depth, breadth and meaning.**

Mindfulness

Positive thinking and mindfulness form part of my style, but only when I am in a resourceful space (which is when I feel that I can be fully present for my client). This is a skill that needs constant practice and reflection. When I reflect back on days when I got myself into a positive frame of mind versus those days when I started off without focusing on my mood, guess which days rendered a better experience for my clients? When working with teams I am always mindful that at any one time I am coaching each individual and the team. The complex dynamics of team coaching bring energy to my being.

This phase consists of a number of sessions and the outcome is a more **consciously competent** client. Clients become more aware of how they present in various situations, acquire the skills to seek feedback from others, reflect thoughtfully and decide on what they need to work on, change or consider, and what they need to learn or unlearn.

Phase 4: implementation and reflection

During this phase, clients implement the learning, reflect on it, share the learning during coaching sessions and decide to embrace (or discard) new skills, thoughts and actions. This personal choice is crucial. They decide what works for them and what doesn't. Clients repeat those behaviours that seem to produce the results they want to achieve, with the learning loop reinforced through feedback, reflection and a coaching environment that offers safety, consideration and a healthy measure of respectful challenge.

The outcomes of this phase are closely related to what was contracted between us. Over and above the outcomes, the self-esteem of clients becomes stronger; they are consciously more competent and some of their newly practised thinking, doing and speaking comes much more naturally than before. The pact already formed between clients and coach is strengthened as clients reach new levels of insight, confidence and performance.

What informs me during this phase, funnily enough, are the theories of conditioning and reinforcement that hail from my days as a practising psychologist. Self-talk and imaging techniques come in very handy during this phase as clients take ownership and embrace progress towards predetermined goals and do so through personal choice.

Phase 5: recognising, appreciating and checking out

This phase overlaps quite a bit with the previous two, since clients go through several rounds of coaching, transformation and implementation, depending on the agreed-upon goals for coaching.

Then the time comes to conclude the coaching journey. This is the part where it is time to say goodbye, however meaningful the relationship may have become. Here it is crucial for me to state my appreciation to the clients for being present and for moving through phases of **forming, storming, norming** and, finally, **performing** around issues; and, also, for being brave enough to consider a new way of thinking, doing, speaking or being. For me, this phase is all about making sure the clients hold the reins of further progress.

My commitment to myself and my clients is to leave them in a resourceful space, knowing that they understand what we have done and how we have done our coaching, leaving them with the key skill of self-coaching. For me to consider my coaching successful, clients should be able to handle future challenges and opportunities similar to the ones addressed during the coaching.

Saying goodbye is not easy. Just like any relationship, coaching has a beginning and an end. Coaches are human, and one of my biggest thrills is a satisfied, self-coaching client. But (and I hate this word **but**), it is all in the contracting. And it is healthy and advisable to contract properly to achieve the best coaching outcomes.

Figure 3.3 illustrates what my coaching model looks like.

Phases 3 to 5 are iterative. During the coaching phase, several coaching "issues" are brought to the table, thought about, experimented with and reflected upon. The client goes forth to "try out" or implement his or her learning. Continuous recognition and appreciation (of the process, each other and the growth) take place. This cycle of activity is represented by the dotted-line triangle in figure 3.3.

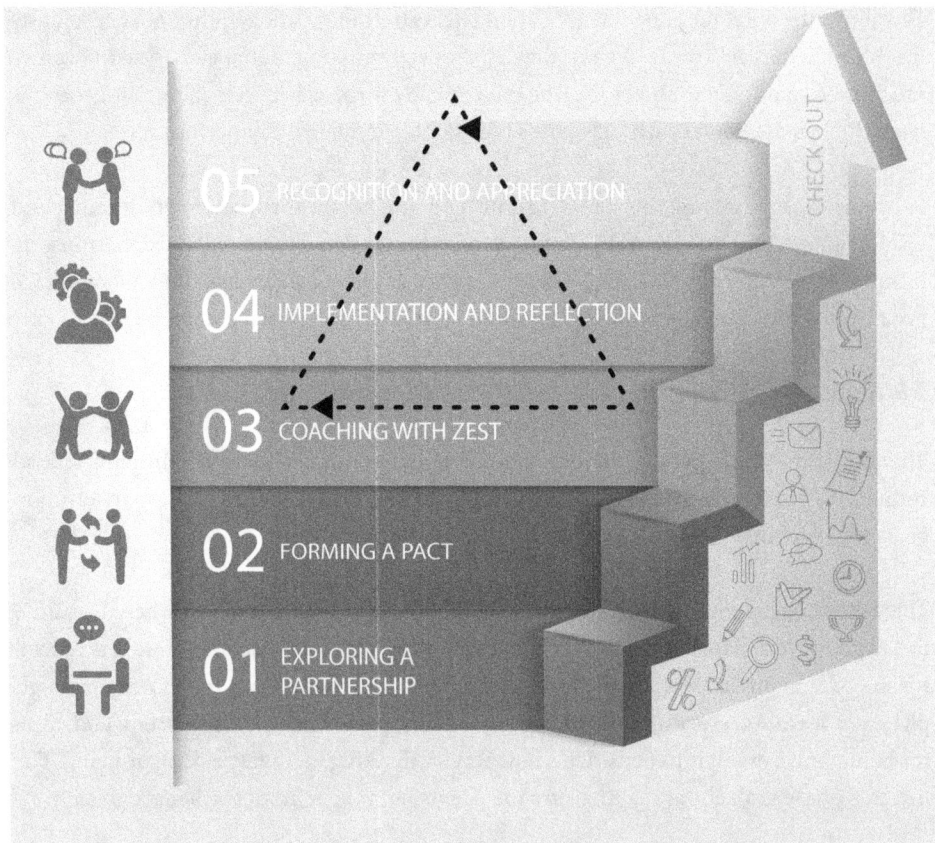

Figure 3.3: A graphic representation of the author's coaching model

LEARNING THEORIES THAT SHAPED MY COACHING APPROACH

In reading about the importance of having a shared concern in *The Impossible Child* by David Lane[51], I recalled an intervention at the school where my child was receiving her formal education. As I have said previously, a shared concern develops when the coach and the contracting or other party begin to examine the areas of concern in any problem situation. Once the issues have been defined it becomes possible to identify aspects that can readily be shared by both parties, thus forming the basis for focused exploration.

An encounter with my child's school principal, which I will describe briefly, represented a real-life example of shared concern. The principal summoned me to her office, saying "Ms van Coller, I am concerned about your child ..." I immediately went to the school, deeply concerned and not fully aware of the situation. When I got to the principal's office, she was forthright about her annoyance and told me that my child was underperforming academically and also had attitudinal problems.

After careful reflection on the behaviours of the stakeholders involved, I realised that what was missing was a shared concern:

- The teacher thought my child was impossible to deal with in the classroom.
- I thought the teacher was incompetent.
- The principal was worried about her new international school and mainly wanted all stakeholders to be happy.
- My daughter was fearful of her teachers, with the result that she withdrew from them.

The school psychologist reported that other children had also been referred to her by the same teacher. The children showed a reluctance to come to school, and reported feeling ill and tense while at school.

With the help of David Lane's guidelines, much prayer and lots of patience and goodwill, we jointly established a forum, which I guided as chair and with my husband as translator. Each party's concerns were explored, after which we agreed on a route to implement and monitor ways to improve the situation. It all turned out very well in the end.

My biggest lesson from this experience is that reality is in the eye of the beholder; until we actually see, understand and are willing to respect each other's viewpoints, we waste time trying to address what we believe the situation to be. More recently, I found resonance in the words of Caren Scheepers about how different roles, once clarified, leverage off one another when a common purpose exists.[52]

Roger Harrison caught my interest with his perception of business as a tutor in competitiveness and action orientation, which are essentially autonomous left-brain activities. His passion was being the tutor of what he calls "love in the workplace"[53]. Harrison's concept immediately captured my imagination, mainly because I share his passion for peace and harmony in organisations. His was not the forced type of "harmony" where people don't dare to speak up when they disagree or are unhappy, but a state of freedom where people can discuss their differences and still feel part of the team.

Harrison dedicated his time and energy as consultant to teaching leaders how to deal with complex living systems such as humans, groups and organisations. The approach essentially requires building nurturing relationships with clients for a willingness to cooperate and an appreciation of the concept of interdependence among such systems. In fact, the reflective notes I made in my copy of his book (which I read in 2003) say, "Be aware of the impact that my client's environment has on his choice, decisions and behaviour", asking the client to explore these in a picture of sorts. After some coaching with one of my very first executive-level clients, another note in the same book reads: "Client himself not aware of these until we coached. Glad I took kokis and flipchart with me, because he drew a decision tree – something he learnt from varsity." What I learnt from this was that it is often through the coaching process itself that a client realises the complexity of his or her environment and the challenges associated with navigating troubled waters.

When I started working with executive teams my reflections on the above expanded even more. I learnt that managerial actions should not be viewed in isolation from the team and the dominant organisational culture. Ignoring the interrelatedness of decisions may detract from the benefit that individualisation holds. An aligned team of leaders understands the power of singing together in their leadership orchestra and they appreciate the contribution that their own voices make to the harmonious sound of the orchestra. They are keenly aware that they are part of the team and at the same time a very special instrument in the ultimate success of the team or teams of which they are part.

On the subject of awareness, John Whitmore[54] sees raised awareness and responsibility as the stepping-stones of a coaching approach that focuses on improved performance. As for team coaching, he advocates a definition of common goals, based on some ground rules to be agreed by the team, to foster cooperation and to move firmly towards the organisational goals.

Management expert Danah Zohar and her husband, the psychiatrist Ian Marshall[55], take alignment to a new level. They assert that much wealth can be created when people's values are aligned with one another while remaining congruent with their own inner spirit. Such wealth nourishes the human spirit and aims to make the future of all humanity sustainable. Roger Harrison[56] agrees. He suggests that in the same way that organisations respond to the demands of customers for more personal service, they should respond to all opportunities by operating from an open heart.

CONCLUSION

This chapter mainly discussed the structure of my personal coaching framework, including perspective, process and purpose. I also discussed the benefits of seeking a shared concern when approaching situations in which the parties involved hold conflicting perceptions. This model, mainly developed for one-on-one coaching, was in the back of my mind when my association with Viking Enterprises kicked off.

The next two chapters share how I guided the executive team of the six independent business units of Viking Enterprises towards the selection of a new organisational culture.

The first part of chapter 4 sets out the context within which I met Viking Enterprises; the second part offers a narrative about my experiences in meeting, greeting and tying the knot! Chapter 5 discusses the actual coaching processes used to achieve the alignment described above.

Chapter 4

FORMING A PACT WITH VIKING ENTERPRISES

INTRODUCTION

At the time this chapter played out in my life, I was busy with a doctorate in coaching. I was armed with an incredible amount of brand-new knowledge, a growing number of coaching hours, the framework and model that I had developed and, most of all, a mind-set of possibility! In this chapter, I want to tell you the story of how I met Viking Enterprises and of my passion for aligning teams of leaders and managers in terms of their thinking, doing and being, not just because they have a vested interest in each other, but also to create sustainable long-term value for those they are accountable to. The first part of this chapter explains the context within which I met my Swedish client/s. The second part offers a narrative about my experiences in meeting the managers and finally "tying the knot" with them. In this chapter I also mention my early reflections and learning, which became essential elements in the coaching process and which are discussed in detail in chapter 11.

Confidentiality and name changes

In discussing my interactions with the organisation mentioned above, I shall call them "Viking Enterprises" in line with a coaching agreement I signed with the executive team of the company. The names used in this book are, therefore, fictitious; I explain the reasons for these name changes in the preface. Nevertheless, the narrative presented here remains factual in every material aspect.

Communication with Viking Enterprises

For the sake of readers who may not be familiar with Scandinavia and its main constituent areas and languages, I start this section with a brief chat about the place in which the proposed coaching project was to be implemented. This was in the locality of Hässleholm in Skåne County, Sweden. The town was small, with a population of about 8 000 at the time I was there in 2004. Six years later, the number had more than doubled to 18 500 people.

Being South African, I speak English and Afrikaans fluently, but I understood little of the Swedish language and its many dialects. So I experienced some early difficulties with effective communication when interacting with the managing director (MD) and his executive team. On a few occasions, I brooded a bit after the meetings and coaching sessions, wondering if all the members had understood exactly what I had been saying even with the help of an interpreter. As a precautionary measure, I began to check their understanding of key issues in subsequent one-on-one sessions.

THE START OF A PARTNERSHIP WITH VIKING ENTERPRISES

During the period 2002 to 2005, I worked, with my Swedish partner, on an international project for the European Union (EU) and the Swedish government with the main aim of setting up a new supply chain for the automotive industry in Scandinavia. The project partnered six totally autonomous companies. The purpose of the project was to reach a working agreement among the six companies leading to participation in the international business arena and, more specifically, to form a new supply chain to serve the automotive industry.

My role in the process was multi-faceted, creating some internal conflict and disadvantages for me at times. I was strategist, negotiator, coach, trainer and facilitator. During the initial phases of this project, I realised that an intensive process of group and individual coaching was the only way to achieve congruency within the group in terms of their particular ways of working. Once I had achieved that state of common understanding – or as we coaches may say, a shared concern – I shifted the focus to training and coaching the key individuals and small teams in the processes of forming new international partners.

Among other things, I had to acknowledge and appreciate the existence of a diverse range of cultural differences; I also had to overcome the language barrier I mentioned earlier. I used coaching, in combination with some training, as the vehicle for the transfer of the new skills. At the time, I saw the dual approach as revolutionary in the field of executive coaching. It worked extremely well for all parties, and the outcomes of that approach were, well ... almost "magical", as one of the executives said.

The project was indeed successful in terms of achieving its aims. Once the new structure was operational it served a key purpose throughout the automotive supply chain, from marketing to the servicing end.

Under the trusted guidance of my partner, many individual elements of the EU project combined exceedingly well to ensure that it was delivered on time, having delivered more than it had set out to do. Looking back on the elements that fostered good cooperation, we realised that commonality in culture and the adoption of a common vision were key prerequisites for success. The stakeholders of the newly formed supply chain agreed that a vision-led plan, which had shared values as its foundation, accounted for much of their focused energy.

The challenge of Viking Enterprises

I became particularly interested in Viking Enterprises because it was undergoing a process of integrating the cultures of its six different business units, involving nine executives who headed these units. The aim of the initiative was for the new company to achieve alignment in its way of thinking and working in order to improve its performance.

Cautiously excited by the success that we had already achieved with the challenging EU project, I pursued Viking Enterprises as my next client, knowing full well that it would present its own unique challenges. On the one hand, a strong mitigating factor was that all the stakeholders were Swedish. On the other hand, the six business units had been decentralised and had adopted distinctively different business cultures. Now the MD, Nielsen Gerhrke (not his real name), wanted one homogenous culture that focused on service. Therein lay the key challenge.

At that point, the preferred culture was little more than a vague concept in the mind of the MD. I felt that he knew he had to do something to reorient his operations and refocus his thinking. However, I also sensed that he did not know how to go about making these changes happen and what the extent of the changes would be. Moreover, it was not very clear in his mind how to achieve his aims.

Viking Enterprises' subcultures and the challenges they posed

The cultures of the various divisions within Viking Enterprises were not aligned in the pursuit of any common vision. There was even a degree of misinterpretation, with different approaches to universal business challenges.

A redeeming feature for me was the successful process we had followed on the EU project, where we had found the congruency we sought and then shifted our attention to training and coaching key individuals and teams in the process of forming new international partnerships. Of course, this progression involved much appreciation of the impacts of cultural differences and language barriers (I conducted all communication with my clients in English). Coaching, in conjunction with needs-specific training, was used to speed up the transfer of new learning.

But perhaps I am getting ahead of myself and need to go back to my first meeting with Viking Enterprises.

Travelling to the first key meeting

On the morning of 24 August 2004, I took the two-hour trip from my Lagernhet apartment to the gracious offices of Viking Enterprises, based at the time in a town called Hässleholm. This would be my first focused meeting with the MD, Nielsen Gerhrke, a man whom I had seen once every two months at the EU coordinating meetings. I had not learnt much about him through those interactions. He was usually thoughtful and quiet, reluctant to participate consistently, except in short bursts and after long intervals. When seated in the EU offices, always in the same seat, I had always felt that he looked small in stature and reserved in nature.

He was a good listener and perhaps more of a doer than a man of many words. His command of the English language was poor, which was probably what inhibited his contributions at the EU meetings. When the deliberations became robust, his input was not exactly extensive. However, when he proffered his views, they sounded logical and well thought out, and were seldom challenged by the group. I discovered that Nielsen impressed colleagues with his profound wisdom. His words were sometimes expressed with a delicate balance between dry humour and intense conviction. "A diamond in the rough" is the expression that comes to mind when I think of him.

On the day of my meeting with Nielsen, and from working with the Viking organisation before, it was clear that Viking's executive team was not aligned in their thinking or conduct. Although it was already a successful company, it had the potential to capture a much larger market share. The question was: Did they see the potential and would they think it worth their while to spend time to get onto the same page with regard to their key challenge? This challenge was, in the words of their MD, "How to align themselves towards one cohesive culture and achieve better customer service ratings and in so doing capture a bigger market share". Would they want to work with me and would they embrace a concept, very new at the time, called team coaching?

Diligence had to be the watchword, so I prepared well for the day. As I approached my destination, a tiny town in the south-west of Sweden, my mind was racing in all directions and I had to focus on being centred. So I opened the car window and felt the cool breeze wafting in from Lake Finja, a mass of water that runs almost parallel with the road all the way from Malmö. It was 20 degrees centigrade, the sun was out and I guess this added to my hope that the meeting would result in a mandate to implement coaching while working with a company in which I truly believed. What spurred me on even more was that I needed the work!

The interview

When I entered the boardroom of Viking Enterprises I found two gentlemen present. They were Nielsen, the MD, and his right-hand man – let's call him Jens. I presented my credentials to them, focusing on my capabilities in terms of professional coaching and explaining the benefits of such coaching processes for any organisation seeking better alignment.

I had prepared a set of questions for the interview, collectively designed to identify the organisational problems, and ultimately to lead to a set of agreed objectives for a new vision and culture. The questions were split into two groups, namely those that concerned company status and those that concerned company culture and values. Jens acted as interpreter. What follows is a verbatim recall of the interview, which is intended to help prepare you for such situations in your future.

Questions on the company status

The formalities over, I asked Nielsen: "Tell me, how is Viking Enterprises performing?"

He answered: "In terms of numbers, Viking Enterprises represents 10% of the people in the group, but we bring in 55% of the turnover. We are moving from an hourly consulting engineering business to a project-orientated business."

Jens relayed the Swedish message almost seamlessly. Still, it soon became a tedious process, and also eerie in some ways. The two men were almost indivisible; a strong bond seemed to exist between them. The level of trust was palpable at first. My faith in Jens's ability to convey the messages correctly was forced by circumstances. I had to trust him implicitly.

I pressed on. My doubts dissipated and soon I was almost fascinated by the understanding I saw between the two senior men. Jens was confident, never hesitant, and seemed to understand exactly what was going on in the head of Nielsen, the man in charge. Watching the interaction, I felt that sometimes Jens appeared to be guessing correctly how Nielsen would respond. The situation was uncanny. At times I got the feeling that Jens was the MD and not Nielsen. Clearly, Nielsen trusted Jens to translate his Swedish message with perfection and the highest level of integrity.

Me: "Nielsen, what future plans do you have for the company?"

Nielsen: "Our aim is to become more project-orientated. Three years ago, 5% of our turnover came from project business and today that figure is about 40%. Our aim is to increase it to 80% of our total turnover in the next three years."

Me: "Do you have a strategy in place to achieve this?"

Nielsen: "Not really. However, we saw the need for this type of change some two years ago when a few major companies left this country. We have made a few structural changes already but much more work is needed. Many of our customers do not understand the change, and I am sure neither do half of our own staff."

Questions on the company culture and values

Me: "Do you believe that companies have culture and value systems?"

Nielsen: "Yes."

Me: "Briefly describe the culture of Viking Enterprises."

Nielsen: "We are trying to change people's minds about our business. We want them to think in project terms and we want to be seen as a customer-orientated entity. I want all the customers of all of our business units to have the same high regard for our service ideals."

Me: "Is there more?"

Nielsen: "We need more repeat business from customers. I want the brand name to be consistently good on all products and projects. That is the culture I want but I am not so very good at these soft issues. I am an entrepreneur, not an implementer of change."

Me: "Do you believe that there is unity among the members of your executive team with regard to such company values?"

Nielsen: "No. They all have different values. Most of them realise that change is necessary, but we have never openly shared our perceptions regarding the current or the preferred cultures of the organisation."

Me: "Do you believe it is possible to reach agreement on new company values?"

Nielsen: "Yes, but I don't feel comfortable dealing with such issues."

Me: "What tangible methods have you tried out or considered doing in this regard?"

Nielsen: "My strategy is mostly in my head. I have to communicate it much better to all the people in the organisation."

Me: "What is in it for the organisation if all members of your executive team find agreement regarding new company values?"

Nielsen: "Hopefully, we shall have consistent standards among all our business units in terms of the way we do business, the quality of our service. Customers will come back for more."

Me: "Have you considered coaching as a vehicle to bring about agreement for new company values?"

Nielsen: "No."

Me: "What is in it for you, Nielsen, should your team agree on coaching and a new vision?"

Nielsen: "I have already told the owner that I am not the type of leader who will take this company forward because I am not so good with changing people or implementing change."

I asked Nielsen if he would consider a change proposal from me. He readily agreed.

Me: "Thank you for your time so far. Let's look at a provisional proposal I have drawn up in the format of a process flow diagram."

I proceeded to explain some cultures, as described by Roger Harrison[57], and presented an overview of Harrison's organisational survey. I then showed them my process flow diagram, which indicated optional routes towards a coaching intervention, supported by training in the area of project management.

Both Nielsen and Jens were excited by the idea that values are the essence of corporate identity and culture. Nielsen's personal belief was that values underpin culture, and that **what a company does** (its business focus) is as critical as **the way in which it is done** (its values and cultural focus).

The meeting was turning out well for all. The company already perceived cultural diversity as the best way to generate a dynamic environment at work. Moreover, Nielsen showed commitment to finding out what their culture should be, and was amenable to using coaching as a tool to do so. The overall business philosophy and goals already reflected strong support for both key values and the individual growth and empowerment of each employee. We agreed that I should meet the full executive team two weeks later.

I took my leave of Nielsen and Jens, thankful that we had an agreement in principle for change management with coaching as the key intervention.

Objectives agreed

After comprehensively fielding the many questions that came with my presentation to the full executive team of Viking Enterprises, agreement from the team was a fitting climax. Then we had to agree again, this time on the next moves. The team was on a roll! The executive team expressed commitment to finding out what their culture should be and agreed to use coaching as a tool to do so.

The team also agreed on the six objectives below, preparatory to determining the preferred organisational culture:

- Confirm with all other employees of the company that they agree to use coaching to facilitate agreement regarding the preferred culture in the organisation.
- Map out the coaching steps developed in the process of facilitating agreement among all members of the executive team regarding the preferred culture for their organisation.
- Use coaching to investigate and determine the indicators to be used to reflect the preferred culture of the organisation.
- Gain insight into perceptions of both the existing and preferred cultures of the organisation from a sample of staff members at lower levels of the organisation.
- Draw up a list of personal and team behaviours that reflects the preferred culture within the organisation.
- Define a set of personal (individual) goals and a set of team goals aimed at leadership practices that would facilitate positive growth towards the development of the preferred culture.

On 8 October 2004, the MD of the client organisation signed an agreement for the implementation of my coaching proposal, which suggested coaching as the tool to reach alignment on the company culture.

The agreement specified the title, aims, outcomes, scope, feasibility and impact of the proposed research. At the stage of reaching agreement with my sponsors on the expected project outcomes, I felt confident about my personal knowledge and the skill levels needed for the successful completion of the project. An example of the agreement that I used has been included in this book for your use and is marked as Appendix A.

Even though I was jubilant, my feet were planted firmly on the ground. I knew the days ahead would be tough. Language might again be a communication hurdle, as I understood little of the Swedish language. And indeed, I did experience some early difficulties with effective communication when interacting with the MD and his executive team at Viking Enterprises.

With the day's work done, I drove home in the near darkness, exhausted but feeling very satisfied with the outcomes of the proceedings.

CONCLUSION

The six objectives above show how effectively coaching may be used to obtain agreement regarding a preferred culture within an executive team. The results achieved through this endeavour may also offer useful guidance to coaches working in the arena of organisational culture.

In chapters 6 and 7 I return to the six objectives mentioned above to provide context and more detail on the discussions, and to relate each one to a specific milestone designed to ensure that the planned process was guided to its intended conclusion.

Chapter 5 discusses the actual coaching processes used to achieve the alignment referred to above, and also examines key business aspects of Viking Enterprises.

Chapter 5

COACHING: ALIGNING CULTURE WITH STRATEGY

INTRODUCTION

Chapter 4 saw me successfully contracting with the executive team of Viking Enterprises to use coaching as the vehicle to achieve alignment within the team. There was agreement on two fronts: firstly, on the preferred culture of the organisation and secondly, on those leadership practices needed to facilitate the development of the preferred culture.

This chapter discusses the actual coaching processes used to achieve the alignment of culture with strategy. The chapter also shows the development of a new vision aimed at improving business performance for Viking Enterprises. In so doing, it examines the key business aspects analysed by its executive team.

THE COACHING MANDATE

The MD of Viking Enterprises was keen to know which management practices had to be put into place to standardise service delivery across all the business units and to ensure repeat business. He expected the outcomes to strengthen the internal organisational brand across all business units.

The mandate was clear. In terms of my formal agreement with Viking Enterprises, I was contracted to:

- Administer a cultural survey to all members of the executive team, as well as to a second group consisting of people at different levels of the organisation. The purpose was to ascertain the perceptions of employees with regard to the four distinct cultures the survey purported to measure.
- Facilitate sessions with the executive team to determine the preferred culture with its values and behaviours.

- Conduct group and individual coaching sessions to establish the existence of any differences between team members about their own perceptions of existing and preferred cultures in the organisation.
- Have reasonable access to key resources (people and information), and communicate openly about the project, its intentions, progress and findings.

The cultural survey was administered to the second group in Viking Enterprises in order to:

- Examine the perceptions of the reigning organisational culture at different levels of the organisation.
- Check the reality of the executive team's perceptions with regard to the research topic.

Stakeholders

The stakeholders of this research project were many and varied. The beneficiary at the time was **Viking Enterprises**, represented by the MD and the nine members of his executive team. Six of the members were heads of geographical business units, each with its own business goals, clients, leadership styles and cultures. The other three members managed support functions. (At the end of this chapter I mention the potential new beneficiaries of this coaching endeavour.)

Coaching sessions

As part of the coaching process, I made transcripts of every individual coaching session. I analysed and reflected on them to confirm individual perceptions of the management and leadership practices that sustained the prevailing culture versus those that would foster the planned new culture.

I used the transcripts and reflections to gain insight into the appropriateness of the various steps in the coaching process and to explore how effectively they supported progress towards agreement on the preferred culture for Viking Enterprises. The transcripts of individual coaching sessions also provided me with essential personal feedback. Firstly, the feedback confirmed that my coaching style was successful. Secondly, I received feedback on my efforts to help members of the executive team establish the meaning of their personal values, as well as understand how those related to the values displayed by the group.

Making meaning through reflection

Reflection became an integral part of my coaching process at Viking Enterprises. Reflection is a series of activities through which we make sense of our experiences, based on our own evidence (our interpretation of what happened). Once we have reflected on any event we are able to better construct our own description of what we felt, thought and experienced.

Through this process of reflection, I discovered a unique perception of the executives' values in terms of beliefs, behaviours, practices, sentiments and feelings, and how these values related to the values of others. I consider personal perceptions critical to a meaningful conversation regarding values. For example, we may say that we appreciate openness, but what does that really mean? All people have their own images of what openness looks like and how openness features as behaviour in their day-to-day dealings with others.

All those people who are expected to work together for the sake of reaching a common goal will find it useful to:

- Reflect on and share what these images of openness look like.
- Decide with which behaviours they identify when it comes to being **open**.

The popular saying that "what gets measured, gets managed" has particular relevance when comparing a current culture with a preferred one within organisations. Rollins and Roberts[58] advise us to compare the values and behaviours that employees experience every day with the culture to which the organisation aspires. Doing so helps us to better understand how the work culture may be improved.

Values and relationships

The journey in which the participants of my project would find meaning and purpose was of special interest to me. I was keen to understand the role played by personal values and relationships (how and why they related to others and, in particular, their response to the culture in which they operated). To discover answers to these matters I found it useful (when focusing on Viking Enterprises) to:

- Map out the process through which agreement would be reached among all members of the executive team regarding the culture, even if it meant having to adopt a combination culture.
- Investigate, by means of coaching, the indicators that reflect the preferred organisational culture.

Agreeing on the relevance of the process

The MD and I readily agreed on my conducting a two-day workshop for all the executives that reported to him. That workshop had two distinct thrusts:

- **Primary focus**: agree on the importance of aligning all stakeholders to the strategy and culture of the organisation
- **Secondary focus**: agree that coaching could play an instrumental role in achieving cultural and value alignment in the organisation, provided the executive team:
    - agreed on the current culture and also on what the preferred culture should look like
    - identified the behavioural indicators that would mobilise all employees towards a newly preferred way of doing business

Aligning culture and strategy

The key message I emphasised throughout the workshop was that strategy is **what** we do in the organisation, while culture is **how** we do business. The two must be in alignment for the organisation to develop a homogeneous way of doing business, especially with regard to the levels of service provided by the various units. Such service uniformity would give customers confidence in the organisation's ability to serve their needs.

At the time, Viking Enterprises had no formal strategic plan in place and so the strategy had to be our starting point. In effect, this meant that I had to postpone the coaching until the team decided on a uniform strategy. That approach followed on from my hypothesis that any decision about any preferred organisational culture has to follow the decision about what strategy to adopt. Strategy must come first, then culture.

The expected outcomes from the two-day event were:

- Develop a common way of thinking about the future strategy of the organisation.
- Develop a strategy based on market intelligence.
- Ensure alignment and agreement on the agreed future of the organisation.

The workshop objectives were achieved by assessing the current strategy against the principles and practices of successful organisations worldwide. We used practical tools to plan, implement and monitor the agreed strategy. On a personal level, the members of the executive team wanted to understand one another's business units better to facilitate closer cooperation.

Team members also showed interest in using one another's strengths in the process of becoming an effective and cohesive team. They quite rightly felt that such an approach would facilitate the bridge-building required to overcome the barriers caused by operating in different geographical areas.

Leadership styles and cultures

After the executive members agreed to venture into team coaching, they began to accept the need to shed those activities that were part of with the dominant control-oriented culture they wanted to change. They shared a desire to unearth those things that would foster a new environment in which internal customers felt eager to perform to higher levels and offer support to others striving for the same goals. In effect, they would risk exposing their innermost thoughts to a personal coach in exchange for honing their leadership behaviour to meet the norms agreed by their individual teams.

I saw the initial movement towards the preferred culture goals. It came from new attitudes and some inspired leadership. It looked slow and halting at first, with different groups responding at different speeds, but there was momentum – and all in the right direction! I knew deep in my heart that the momentum would mobilise every employee towards an organisational culture that would bring greater success to the company, to the benefit of all members.

Figure 5.1 shows the elements and the process involved in deciding upon a new business strategy.

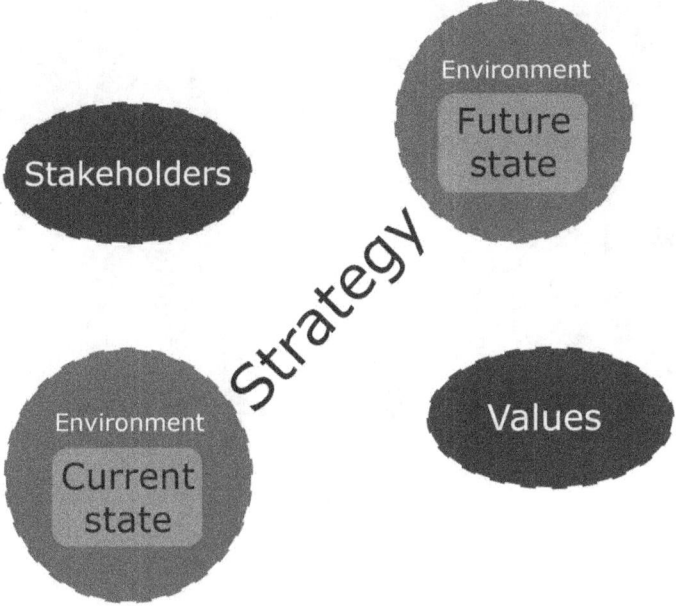

Figure 5.1: How a business strategy is decided[59]

Future state and environment

Firstly, the future state of the organisation was determined, after which the environment of the envisioned future state was described. The same was done with the current state of affairs in order to determine the gap between targeted business results or outcomes, and those currently being achieved. In so doing, the expectations of all relevant stakeholders – such as customers, shareholders, suppliers and staff – were taken into account, as well as the key values underpinning the organisation going forward.

The executive team was unanimous in their resolve to leave behind what seemed to be a control-oriented organisational culture for one that accommodated greater diversity. This process culminated in a statement of intent, or a strategic purpose and direction for Viking Enterprises. The next step was to analyse the wider business environment to identify business opportunities and threats. Figure 5.2 illustrates the three analytical tools used to determine the strategy:

- the PESTLE analysis technique
- a market analysis tool
- the 7S theory

Figure 5.2: Mapping out the business environment[60]

The outer ring in figure 5.2 represents the PESTLE analysis technique used to scan the global business environment in terms of the opportunities and threats in the political, economic, social, technological, environmental and legal arenas.[61]

The inner circle represents a market analysis tool borrowed from Porter,[62] and the middle block hosts the 7S theory used to assess the organisation's internal readiness to implement a newly decided strategy, referring to the organisation's management style, strategy, structure, systems, staff, skills and shared values.[63]

Journalling my findings

My journal contained learning points and reflections on significant events throughout all workshops and all coaching sessions. This enabled me to reflect daily on my notes made during each intervention, and also to reflect on my reflection-in-action later on. I was guided by the journal specifically to remind myself of the role that I should be playing and the ethical standards I had set for myself, and to ensure that I remained true to my own coaching framework, values and ethical standards. Moreover, the reflections guided me in choosing the focus, direction and aim of the next intervention.

The reflections of the members I coached were treated with the utmost sensitivity and confidentiality – I used them mainly to determine the accuracy of my own reflections. Their experiences regarding process, style and progress were explored too. I found that each participant's diary or feedback revealed his or her perspective on events and the feelings he or she held in relation to them. I also thought that the feedback generated valuable insights into the coaching process itself.

A NEW VISION STATEMENT

An analysis completed during one of the workshops was used to determine a new organisational vision statement, using the key ingredients of a good value statement, namely:

- what the company does
- the markets in which it operates or aims to operate
- what the competitive advantage is
- how well the company is doing in the market
- how well it applies all of its resources
- how it does business
- how strong the economic viability of the company is

The newly agreed vision statement for Viking Enterprises therefore read as follows:

Viking Enterprises:

- offers technical services and total engineering solutions to manufacturing industries for projects of all sizes, including turnkey projects and engineering services
- operates in close proximity to our customers
- is open to all markets where we can use and continually develop our existing exceptional competence in both engineering and project delivery
- is open to networking and partnering with our international counterparts, with a view to strengthening and developing long-term, viable customer relationships
- ensures an uncomplicated business experience that provides a mutually beneficial business result/outcome for all involved

The application of the tools illustrated in figure 5.2 led to the identification of the strengths, weaknesses, opportunities and threats (SWOT) impacting on the organisation at the time. It is worth mentioning that these elements played a key role in determining the preferred culture. The market environment in which Viking Enterprises operated at the time is depicted in figure 5.3:

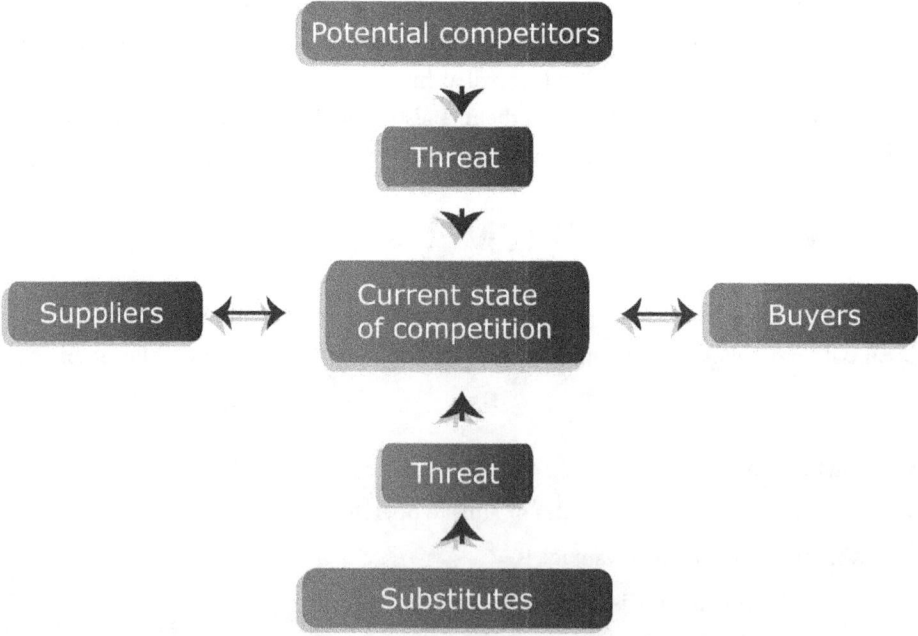

Figure 5.3: The market environment[64]

The executive team also scrutinised the following five environmental factors:

- risks posed by new entries as potential competitors
- degree of rivalry among established companies
- bargaining power of buyers
- bargaining power of suppliers
- threat of substitute products

The two days of the workshop were tough and arduous at times. Every contribution was carefully considered. The closing conversation centred around the need for a consistent culture that would ensure that whenever any Viking Enterprises customer does business with any of its units, that customer receives the same consistently high standard of service.

SETTING AND PLANNING TEAM GOALS

Every group coaching session ended with a team goal plan that underlined the need for management and leadership practices to provide focus for the individual coaching sessions. For example, it may have seemed that a support culture was preferred but there was a lack of recognition for work well done (a supportive leadership practice). In such cases the team explored ways to circumvent apparent contradictions. A resolution was passed at the end of the group coaching session, urging team members to explore new ways to overcome similar challenges with their own staff.

My individual coaching sessions that followed provided opportunities for team members to examine their resourcefulness, willingness and ability to recognise the efforts of subordinates.

The executive team was able to meet only for half a day once a month to explore a preferred culture on which all members could agree. This was followed up by one or two coaching sessions per person during the rest of the month, to explore individual readiness to display the leadership practices adopted during the team session.

In total, six cycles of group coaching followed by individual coaching sessions were arranged, where each cycle represented a milestone. I played two roles during every coaching session – that of facilitator and that of group coach. The facilitator role ensured that sufficient progress was made at every group session towards a goal predetermined by the group. However, the more important role was that of team coach, where I created an environment that stimulated free and honest expression.

The setting up and achievement of the agreed milestones are discussed in chapters 6 and 7.

The outcomes of group coaching sessions were logged and reflected upon to ensure that every member of the team was in agreement with the decisions made in these sessions. Of course, every member had to be actively involved in this part of the process. I collated the information and used it to reflect on my objectivity, my coaching approach and my ethical conduct. It also guided my decisions around the next steps in the process. My focus was almost single-mindedly on reaching unanimous agreement on matters relating to a preferred culture.

The outcomes and reflections on group coaching sessions were used to confirm indicators (behaviours, sentiments, practices and beliefs) of a specific culture. All the indicators reflecting the existing and preferred cultures therefore assumed great relevance. My probing for confirmation helped to achieve one of the main aims of the research project – that of fostering alignment among the executive team members regarding a preferred organisational culture and leadership practices.

Questionnaire: Harrison and Stokes

Harrison and Stokes[65] give numerous accounts of successful projects of this kind, using their questionnaire to diagnose organisational culture. At Viking Enterprises, the data gathered through the questionnaire was used to provide impetus to both the group and individual coaching sessions throughout the project processes. It achieved the aims of:

- gaining insight into the existing and preferred cultures of the organisation, as perceived by staff members on lower levels of the organisation
- defining a list of personal and team indicators and behaviours which would eventually reflect the preferred culture within the organisation

The questionnaire was administered to the entire executive team, and lower down the hierarchy to randomly selected representatives. This sampling method was considered best for identifying perceptions at various levels throughout the organisation. It was highly desirable to determine variances between the executive team and the remainder of the staff members and to quantify the extent of those differences in perception.

CONCLUSION

Having identified a need for a stronger focus on customer service, the executive team of Viking Enterprises was eager to embark upon a journey of discovery. The overriding aim of the team was to stimulate higher levels of organisational, team and personal achievement, supported by practices that would foster higher levels of service between internal and external customers.

The grand plan was for the executive team to identify the dominant current culture and select a preferred one for their organisation. The instrument for achieving this was the Harrison and Stokes Diagnostic Questionnaire in combination with group discussions. Although the individual leadership style of each member was different, all shared the need to abandon the control-oriented organisational culture. They all wanted a new culture that could unite a diverse combination of cultures and promote shared decision-making.

With direction from me, the process progressed beyond the point of agreement regarding a preferred culture to agreeing on a set of workable leadership practices. Moreover, each of the practices had to be executed by every member of the team in a collective effort to facilitate the preferred culture.

Once implemented, the new beneficiaries of this project will be:

- teams of leaders and managers around the world who struggle with issues of alignment. I particularly target those who are not sure of the dominant values and culture of their organisations, and who do not know precisely what constitutes a certain culture or how it should be lived.
- coaches and prospective coaches who have to work within the boundaries of company systems and cultural dynamics
- those involved with drawing up practical leadership behaviours to reflect a given culture that could be pursued
- the coaching community at large, who could benefit from a successful research project that focused on a group and individual coaching approach for aligning cultural perceptions
- South Africa, my home country, which presents any coach with profound challenges when it comes to agreeing on values and culture, given that every one of the 11 official language groups is striving for greater acceptance and credibility.

The next two chapters reveal the actual project that facilitated the desired alignment.

Chapter 6

SETTING THE KEY MILESTONES

INTRODUCTION

As I have documented in previous chapters, the executive team of Viking Enterprises took the decision to instil a new culture, mainly for a stronger focus on customer service. This goal was supported by the divisional managers, who diligently pursued higher levels of return by concentrating on customer satisfaction that targeted both internal and external customers.

Accordingly, this chapter explains the six objectives (or milestones on the journey) and how they were planned, while the next chapter discusses how they were achieved.

WHY SOME INITIATIVES FAIL

My reflections on why projects fail in spite of commitment from top leaders led me to the belief that stakeholders who were not part of the original decision to change things do not understand the context within which the decision was taken. Consequently, they are unable to relate the change to a future vision.

Good leaders have the capacity to envision a situation sometime in the future. What they often forget is that not everybody has this ability. Some people are by nature able to see, think and comprehend only a short time into the future. When I coach leaders with an amazing ability to create a vision, I often find that it helps to remind them that they have to make their vision more accessible. I suggest they do this by breaking their long-term vision into smaller parts and finding the right words to describe it and the best pictures to illustrate it. In so doing, their chances of reaching their audience (all other associates in the organisation) are enhanced. This, to my mind, is buy-in! Only when we are able to see what others see and believe can there be successful buy-in.

The leaders of each of the six business units and their head offices were perceived as stakeholders, as well as every person who reported to them, including all suppliers and customers. Moreover, the change process had to be clearly understood, particularly at the level of the executive team.

To emphasise the reality that nothing is guaranteed without a concerted team effort, I opened a discussion with the executive team on why some organisations have failed with their change management interventions. All the while, I led the session carefully to set a tone for achieving the purpose of the organisation. Painting a vision was a prerequisite – a vision that would elicit participation and produce a conversation of urgency and with varying viewpoints. I knew that at times I had to play the role of devil's advocate, and even create some anger and discomfort, to solicit inputs of value.

As a starting point for my address to the executive members, I related a case study of an international company situated in Denmark. Its leader believed that we often explain away failed business initiatives in rational and structural terms instead of focusing on the values and perceptions of the leaders of such initiatives. That Danish organisation engaged a coaching psychologist to help the organisation achieve a turnaround. It was really a process where communication, creativity, cooperation and business ethics were consciously developed among the leaders of the organisation. The rationale behind the process was that if leaders could trust each other implicitly and show mutual respect through open communication, the new culture would (and in fact, did) filter down throughout the organisation.

I gave the Viking Enterprises executive team members time out to reflect on the case. Their assignment for the afternoon was for each one to phone two or three customers and get some understanding of how these customers viewed the culture of Viking Enterprises (their way of working, treating customers and building relationships). When we convened the next day, discussion was robust, energetic and animated. Everybody had done the homework and could not wait to share their feedback. The session was rounded off with time for reflection, followed by feedback on what they felt would be the key elements that would make for a successful culture change initiative.

The following viewpoints reflect some of the feedback given by the team members to help set the scene for designing milestones for success:

- It is critical to take a holistic view of the business situation, that is, of the internal business environment and the external competitive environment and all stakeholder relations, before defining the milestones of the project.
- It is imperative that the executive team members agree on the preferred culture of the organisation in a way that also offers clarity on what is required to achieve it.

- Everyone needs to know how success will be measured and how they will be supported in their efforts to change.
- The change initiative must be framed as a formal project, to provide a structure that is understandable to everyone involved.

The team had prepared well. The point on project management pleased me immensely, as the suggestion totally supported my project approach to the alignment of a leadership team regarding the preferred culture and leadership practices. Viking Enterprises was an engineering firm and related well to project management. For this reason, the team agreed to use a project approach to the intervention complete with milestones, objectives and measurement.

Another of the key points related to communication: multi-directional communication was considered essential for success. Misconceptions about intentions and a lack of proper communication with stakeholders would result in resistance to the initiative.

My response to the above challenge was that the team-coaching approach would make a significant difference where effective communication systems were put in place. The team agreed on the issues to be addressed, decided on the outcomes and agreed on the following process:

- team coaching, followed by
- one-on-one coaching for all senior managers

This particular process was crucial for me, as coach, to provide support for the new learning, key reflections and shifts in thinking, and the kinds of behaviour that had to be demonstrated to the rest of the people in the organisation.

One of the members pointed out that is useful to view a change in leadership style from a perspective of capability, perhaps stating what is obvious and yet is critical for successful change management interventions. He said that managers need to plan to overcome resistance to change, particularly when introducing new processes or strategic approaches. In this regard, planning and communication are critical for minimising resistance to letting go of the old and doing new things.

Everyone in the room agreed with this viewpoint and we decided that the best way to overcome resistance to change is to develop a vision – in this case, the new organisational culture – agreed by all stakeholders. They also welcomed some one-on-one coaching when they realised that embracing a new culture would inevitably prompt the unlearning of old habits and the learning of new ones, relating to ways of thinking, doing and especially being.

The section that follows describes the milestones set for the process to achieve the agreement of a preferred organisational culture for Viking Enterprises.

Milestone 1: Reaching agreement on the coaching process

Milestone 1 was to confirm the use of coaching to facilitate agreement with the team and also with all other employees of the company regarding the preferred culture in the organisation.

You will recall that part of the purpose of my first interview with the MD was to determine his needs and expectations regarding an intervention intended to "align the various business units in the organisation", as he put it. The second aim of that interview was to determine the readiness of the MD and his team to embark on a journey to define the culture that would facilitate business unity among the nine executives in the business units of the organisation.

When I asked the MD about his definition of alignment, it became clear that he expected customer-oriented and project-focused behaviour. Once it was established that he would consider coaching as an intervention, I provided an overview of the four cultures described by Harrison and Stokes[66]. I also presented the authors' organisational survey, which is described in chapter 5.

We then discussed a process flow diagram that I had prepared, to show a route toward the implementation of a coaching intervention. It was agreed that a phenomenological approach would be followed, distilling a sequence of steps necessary to achieve the main aims of the project. That process would also inform Milestone 2 on the journey, being the development of an organisational strategy for the client.

I used English as a medium throughout the process, including all of the coaching sessions, and must confess to having had some reservations about the one-on-one coaching of the MD due to his limited grasp of English. I feared that any inadequate understanding of my questions would taint the validity of his responses and thus that of the research. The probability was high that our coaching relationship would be difficult, and if so, our conversations would not render the best results possible. The MD proposed that his second-in-command (2IC) sit in on my coaching sessions with him to help with translation when necessary. I agreed to this approach.

Chapter 6: Setting the key milestones

> Having learnt much about ethics and the importance of confidentiality in building solid rapport based on trust and so on, I felt slightly uncomfortable about the language difficulty. Yet I accepted that it was crucial for the MD's views, feelings, concerns and challenges to be voiced, listened to and understood. It meant that I trusted that the 2IC would be completely honest and also accurate in relating his leader's words in Swedish to me in English. What if something got lost in translation? How would I know when this was happening?
>
> I was determined to reflect on this experience as part of my learning journey, and I offer you my reflections in chapter 11 of this book.

The key objective of this session was to probe and agree on the need for consistency in the way all employees believed they should behave towards customers in all the business units. Using the outcomes of the earlier interview with the MD, I presented my agreement to the core executive team, proposing that coaching be the vehicle. This is covered in a previous chapter.

The Gantt chart I had prepared (a common project management tool used to ensure timely completion) showed the planning of all six milestones.

The signed agreement – Milestone 1 – signified the official start of my research project. We adjourned the meeting with a commitment to have a sensitising session for the complete executive team during the following week, with the aim of stimulating their thought processes regarding concerns about current business practices and stakeholder satisfaction. The meeting also agreed on the urgent need to decide upon an organisation-wide business strategy.

As I had not yet come to know all members of the executive team personally, I had little sense of what they knew about aligning businesses, or even how they felt about the subject. I thus used a facilitative style of engagement with a strong educational undercurrent. This approach was informed by the need to be able to analyse and decide on the strategic direction for the business units and the company as a whole. My educational role was to facilitate that understanding. I had to secure agreement for alignment within the executive team against the background of how business should be conducted and how customers should be served. The key message was my underlying belief that strategy is **what we do**, while culture represents **how we do it**.

The outcome of the sensitising session was agreement on the following actions to enhance business conduct and business results:

- Align themselves faster to offer customers what they wanted.
- Explore which individual and company values would facilitate alignment in the way in which business is done and how values are represented.
- Revisit the existing vision of Viking Enterprises. It was not practical enough to be understood by all, nor had it been communicated well to all stakeholders.
- Develop a revised strategy with a new vision for capturing new markets and better serving current and future clients. It had to be something that everyone in the company could buy into.
- Have a strategic intervention serving as Milestone 2, after which the existing and preferred cultures could be determined and clearly defined.

Milestone 2: Developing an organisational strategy

This milestone was set to map out the steps developed in the process of facilitating agreement among all members of an executive team regarding the preferred culture.

After the sensitising session, the strategic plan was the next priority, after which we planned to resume the cultural alignment process. The reasoning behind this decision was twofold:

- A new vision and strategy was uppermost in the minds of the executive team and was therefore a business matter that demanded priority.
- Formulating a strategy that all the stakeholders believed in preceded decisions about a preferred culture.

In terms of the process, I had to deal with the reality of the limited time I was to spend with the organisation.

I knew that helping the organisation with its new vision and strategy would eat into my time to do the project. Yet I could not see myself doing work on culture when the client did not have a clear strategy. All of my learning and experience to that point had convinced me that culture facilitates strategy and that strategy has to be determined first. To my mind, strategy defines **what** a company was about to do while culture defined **how** it was to be done. There was no way I could continue with my project until Viking Enterprises had a vision and strategy for its business.

Since I had good rapport with them, I agreed to help with the process of defining their new vision and strategy. We decided to put the coaching project on hold to focus on reaching consensus on this definition. For this reason, no further mention will be made of the strategic intervention, other than the fact that it constituted Milestone 2 on the Gantt chart and that the team used the BSC to devise the core strategic drivers and measurements of the organisation.

Milestone 3: Sharing perceptions

This milestone was set to allow the executive team to:

- Unearth employee perceptions of the current culture and how the new preferred culture should look.
- Gain insight into the perceptions of both the existing and preferred cultures of the organisation through a representative sample of staff members at lower levels.
- Investigate and determine the indicators that would reflect the preferred culture of the organisation.

This phase of the project saw the application of the organisational culture questionnaire by Harrison and Stokes[67], which I introduced to you in an earlier chapter. The intent was to stimulate thinking around the issue of culture and what really constitutes organisational culture. The strength of this tool is to make culture more practical and understandable by linking it to behavioural indicators.

The questions posed in the questionnaire were instrumental in causing team members to reflect on both team and individual behaviours. The reflections offered a workable starting point for meaningful coaching conversations; the subject and results are discussed in chapter 7. The questionnaire is the intellectual property of the authors; it is therefore not included in this book.

The remainder of this chapter shows the evolution of a process which resulted in the entire executive team agreeing on the combination of cultures they preferred to have in the organisation, which really reflected the attainment of the overall goal of the project.

The application of the organisational culture survey

The following two steps occurred during Milestone 3:

- Apply and score the organisational culture survey with the executive team.
- Apply and score the organisational culture survey with a representative group of other people within the organisation.

In both steps, team members themselves applied and scored the survey, after which the results were displayed on a board for all to see. The main issues were highlighted – those which constituted agreement, as well as those areas where disagreement was apparent. After a brief discussion the session was adjourned, with members well informed about the survey results and having time to contemplate individually what they meant.

The focus at that point was on the survey results of the executive team. The organisational culture survey was later also completed by a representative sample of employees to discover if the organisation's thinking was the same throughout, or different in places, regarding both current and preferred organisational culture.

Survey results of the executive team and the representative group

In essence, this process compared the thoughts of the leaders with the thoughts of others in the organisation regarding the culture survey. Having had to provide feedback with regard to the survey results, I reported that in this step both teams had gained better insight into their own scores versus the scores of the other team (where both current and preferred organisational cultures were concerned). Both teams also became more aware of others' perceptions of the organisation's culture.

In the next chapter, I show how the two teams compared in terms of their respective views of the reigning organisational culture and what they hoped it would eventually be like.

Establishing the main points of agreement

This phase of the project ended with the executive team members agreeing that their current organisational culture is characterised by a combined control-oriented and role-oriented culture. They also agreed that, in future, they would prefer a combined culture that was both achievement-oriented and support-oriented.

Milestone 4: Determining variances between current and preferred cultures

This milestone set out to define a list of personal and team behaviours that would reflect the preferred culture within the organisation.

Reaching this milestone involved the following steps:

- Step 1: Identify the most significant variances between the current and preferred organisational cultures of the client organisation.
- Step 2: Agree on the critical leadership practices that would constitute the preferred culture of the client organisation.

Through team coaching, an agreement was reached to develop 12 leadership and management practices considered feasible to move the organisational culture from focusing on control and roles to focusing on achievement and support. The 12 practices are shown in table 7.1.

The executive team unanimously decided to focus on three issues per month. We only had four months left until the end of the project and 12 issues were yet to be addressed. They felt that team coaching, followed by individual coaching sessions, was essential to reach agreement on how the leadership and management indicators should be dealt with. The group would then give attention to how individual team members perceived their personal needs, and gauge their willingness to modify their behaviour towards the agreed outcomes.

I probed the key variances highlighted in Step 1, first in a team coaching setting and then during one-on-one coaching sessions. The results are discussed in the next chapter of this book.

Milestone 5: Coaching for improved leadership practice

This milestone was set to define a list of personal and team behaviours that would reflect the preferred culture within the organisation.

Milestone 5 introduced steps into the process that facilitated insight into team and individual perceptions of the behavioural indicators reflecting the preferred culture. A key factor was the executive team's informed consent to work on the 12 key leadership challenges. More specifically, they wanted guidance on what to do to provide the type of leadership that would constitute the preferred organisational culture.

The challenges were immense. As the coach, I had to be instrumental in this task of bridging the gap between knowing which culture they wanted and setting goals for the required behaviours. To do this I explored the relevant beliefs, behaviours and constructs underpinning the key leadership challenges. This approach established another level of the agreement: those indicators (feelings, thoughts and behaviours) that demonstrated preferred leadership practice.

The same questions with which the organisational questionnaire probed the preferred organisational culture were used to probe perceptions of how the organisation could foster those leadership practices that would represent the preferred culture. I did this during the one-on-one coaching sessions with each team member.

To be able to achieve the above task within the four months remaining for this project, the executive team agreed on a coaching matrix consisting of four cycles with one day of team coaching to be followed by individual coaching sessions for every member of the executive team.

The first cycle of team coaching started with one of the team members enquiring about the code of conduct that was vaguely in practice but not yet formalised in writing. Such a document is known to be a prerequisite for working teams to function harmoniously. After much discussion, it was decided that the team should draft an official code of conduct to guide behaviour and facilitate teamwork.

Every team meeting would begin with this code to develop a supportive working environment within which results could be achieved. The agreed code represented behaviours from mainly a supportive and achievement-oriented culture (the seemingly preferred combination of cultures for Viking Enterprises), and thus reinforced the team's awareness of behaviours that would reflect the preferred culture throughout the team's coaching day.

The MD suggested that members of smaller work teams who felt able and interested should each volunteer to steer an issue. In this way smaller groups could learn to work together. This move was intended to address one of the organisation's biggest challenges, that of achieving good teamwork. All accepted the suggestion.

An important condition of this process was that every one of the 12 leadership issues should be facilitated in a different small team to avoid the issue of clique formation, an undesirable feature of the reigning organisational culture. Also, the progress on every issue addressed would be presented at each team coaching session. This gave the rest of the members the opportunity to give input or clarify concerns and to be involved in all the issues at hand.

This selective approach produced faster progress than would have been the case had all members taken part in every discussion. Members started to work across traditional barriers. Because of the geographic spread over two provinces, members also learnt to make use of a variety of communication channels, of which teleconferencing and face-to-face meetings were the most popular.

Priorities were attached to the 12 practices to use available project time to the fullest. It was agreed that challenges 1 to 3 would be brainstormed on the first team coaching day, followed by challenges 4 to 6 during the second coaching cycle, with challenges 7 to 9 reserved for the third cycle and 10 to 12 for the last cycle.

Table 6.1: Summary of planned sequencing for priority challenge practices

The priority challenge practices	When to be addressed	Comments
1 to 3	First team coaching day	
4 to 6	Second coaching cycle	
7 to 9	Third coaching cycle	
10 to 12	Final coaching cycle	

Our planning proved overly ambitious, since some issues took longer to address than others and we ultimately dealt with only 11 of the 12 issues (of which the 11th received only minor attention and commitment).

This is how we organised days for team coaching:

- The company code of conduct was revisited to ensure that behaviours focused on achievement and provided support to other team members who needed help.
- The three priority issues allocated to the team coaching sessions were put forward, allowing members to volunteer to take part in discussions on one of the issues. Because the team had a limited number of members and because of their simultaneous involvement in many of the key issues, ample cross-pollination occurred when members worked in more than one team.
- The leadership of each small team remained the same throughout the process to ensure focus, responsibility and progress.
- Each small team brainstormed any shortcomings of the leadership issue at hand. They did so in terms of the current culture, and established leadership and management behaviours they felt were essential to facilitate moving to the preferred culture.
- Each team presented its findings and listened carefully to inputs from the other groups. This process guided each small team towards researching the matter further (outside of the group) and then reporting back at the next team meeting.

The individual coaching sessions that followed every team coaching session offered team members the necessary support to explore their own needs and the resourcefulness to reconsider their own behaviour towards the preferred organisational culture. Coaching sessions were voice-recorded and then transcribed for record-keeping and personal reflection by all.

As the first cycle of coaching came to an end, I noted the reluctance of individual team members to make reflective entries in their journals during the coaching sessions. I asked them to reflect later on the following aspects instead:

- the usefulness of each session
- the coach's style and approach
- the complete process and its potential for ensuring closer cooperation among team members
- any ideas, concerns or needs they may have about progress
- actions, observations, reflections and conversations that should be dealt with **before** the next coaching session
- what they wanted to discuss at the next coaching session

It became apparent that each complete coaching cycle (team coaching followed by individual coaching) brought greater awareness of the leadership and management behaviours likely to foster the preferred organisational culture. I found it reassuring to recognise meaningful shifts in the perceptions of individual responsibility and resourcefulness in fostering the preferred culture of achievement and support.

Milestone 6: Setting goals to facilitate the preferred culture

This milestone aimed to develop a set of personal practices and a set of leadership practices that would facilitate positive growth towards the development of the preferred culture.

In the fourth and last coaching cycle, which culminated in Milestone 6, it was agreed that this stage of coaching should end with a team plan, and also one for each manager of the business units. The plans contained commitments to the practices that would foster growth towards the new organisational culture. This phase of the project signified a planned synthesis of the pledges, personal and team insights and reflections made throughout the process.

I would have been satisfied with a simple code of conduct to present the desirable behaviours to which all members subscribed. However, the team went much further. They created a link from cultural goals (goals to keep reinforcing the preferred culture of support) to strategic goals on the same BSC sheet. They had one for the team (representing the company's plan) and one for individual members of the executive team, representing the business units.

Effectively, this meant that they had mentally integrated **what needs doing** (the strategy) and **how things need to be done** (the preferred culture). These would be put into one document and communicated to all stakeholders inside the organisation to help steer progress beyond this point.

Reaching this milestone would see the successful attainment of the sixth and final one, namely that of defining a set of personal goals and a set of team goals.

These goals jointly aimed at implementing the leadership practices that would facilitate positive growth towards the development of the executive team's preferred culture. This is depicted in figure 6.1.

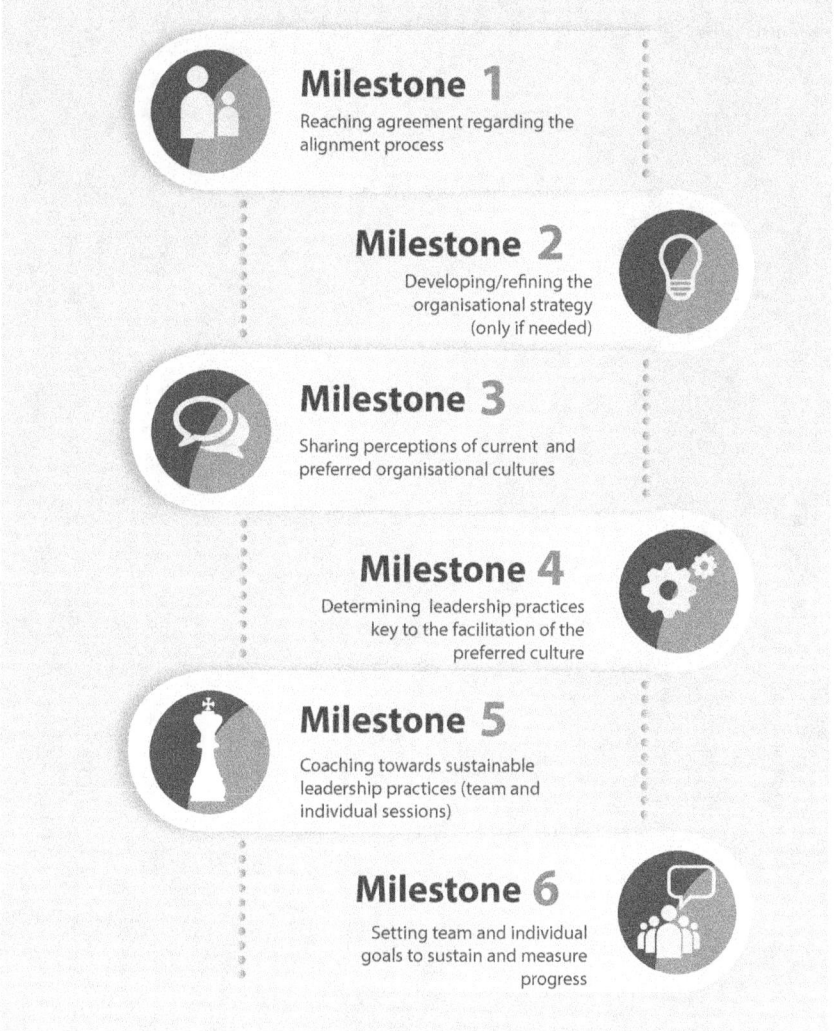

Figure 6.1: The milestones reached by Viking Enterprises

I felt that it was most certainly a job well begun.

CONCLUSION

The project was completed with one final team coaching day during which the MD and every member of the executive team presented the scorecards for which they were accountable, complete with strategic and cultural goals. We agreed to have a follow-up session a year later to measure the culture and to assess progress towards the preferred organisational culture. In fact, the follow-up only happened four years later, with results that were positively astonishing. But there is more about this in chapter 8.

The next chapter details the results of both the individual and group coaching processes and explains how the six milestones set here were met.

Chapter 7

MEETING THE KEY MILESTONES THROUGH A COMBINED COACHING PROCESS

INTRODUCTION

The previous chapter explained the six milestones required to determine a preferred culture for Viking Enterprises. The focus was on how the milestones had been planned and set.

This chapter details the content of the coaching sessions in which agreement was developed among the executive team members of Viking Enterprises on their preferred organisational culture. The emphasis is on the results from both individual and group coaching processes. For easier understanding, the structure of this chapter is similar to the structure used in chapter 6.

The six milestones, as the key objectives, formed the backbone of this project. In fact, the extent to which the milestones were met really became the connecting tendons to guide the coaching process. The content of the coaching conversations became the blood vessels that carried oxygen and energy to the heart of the client – the executive team of Viking Enterprises.

 ## Milestone 1: Reaching agreement on the coaching process

At the outset of this milestone, we had set out to confirm the use of coaching to facilitate agreement with the team regarding the preferred culture in the organisation with the executive team, and also with a second group comprising employees from various levels of the organisation. I conducted buy-in coaching conversations with every member of the executive team and, drawing on the earlier two-day session with the MD and his 2IC, reached agreement with the team members that the project would indeed add value to the organisation.

The aims of the coaching sessions were:

- Bring about clarity on the process of cultural alignment.
- Define the resources needed to implement the process.
- Gain commitment and sustain support for the process to facilitate start-up.

What the team wanted

When probed, the executive team said that they wanted a culture that valued the strengths of every member and the contributions of the staff representing the various business units. They also wanted a closer relationship with one another, and believed that proximity would result in goodwill leading to new business opportunities.

The team also indicated that they would know that a common culture existed among all business units of their organisation once the following indicators became evident:

- stronger teamwork
- better communication
- less blame behaviour
- more sharing of business opportunities
- more income being generated

The most common responses to a question posed on the personal gain people expected showed a need for personal development through better insight into their own behaviour when leading others. I asked: "What benefits do you see for the organisation through participation in this process?" and was told in reply:

- a strong need for the current culture of small-group alliances to be replaced by teamwork
- alignment in terms of the direction the business should follow
- better recognition of team member efforts
- a stronger commitment to one another and the overall goals of the organisation

Coaching as the vehicle

Coaching as the vehicle to be used to reach agreement on the preferred organisational culture received an overwhelmingly positive response, and gave me much hope for the success of the learning journey that lay ahead.

Confidentiality

My crucial questions about confidentiality and ethics showed that most members did not want their responses made known to anyone outside the coaching relationship. They understood that I needed to draw overall conclusions after each round of one-on-one coaching sessions to provide momentum to the process and focus to the group coaching sessions. They gave full and confident permission.

In terms of the confidentiality agreement, transcripts of voice recordings of individual coaching sessions cannot be included in this book – only the coach's summary and reflections have been used. The summary is covered in chapter 11, where my own learning and reflections are discussed for the benefit of anyone wanting to roll out this coaching process.

Milestone 2: Developing an organisational strategy

The second milestone was to map out the coaching steps that had been developed in the process of facilitating agreement among all members of the executive team regarding the preferred culture.

This phase of the project saw the development of a company strategy, complete with vision and mission statements, business unit strategies and, very importantly, a new code of conduct. This part of the project is detailed in chapter 5, with a BSC method used to present the strategy. To my delight, Viking Enterprises realised that its strategic (**to do**) goals and cultural (**how to do**) goals had to be part of its BSC for all of the goals to be taken seriously and receive the focus they deserve.

The BSC presentation, marked Appendix B, is included at the back of this book.

The new code of conduct mandated me to maintain focus and to generate constructive inputs from team members. At this stage they were still very individualistic in their thinking, and unsure of how much openness with me was safe. They all still had the success of their own business units uppermost in their minds.

I highlighted the key provisions of the code at the start of each group session, and focused on behaviours such as communication, meeting management and taking responsibility for commitments made. This was the first time that team members had made such commitments to one another in terms of behavioural conduct. It was thus a significant step in the pursuit of a preferred culture, even before it was known what form this culture would take.

See Appendix C for the code of conduct.

Milestone 3: Sharing perceptions

It was crucial to gather and compare perceptions held by the executive team and staff members at lower levels of the organisation with regard to both current and preferred cultures within the organisation. The questionnaire of Harrison and Stokes[68], introduced in chapter 5, was completed by the two groups. Once scored, the questionnaires rendered valuable insights into the current and preferred cultures of the organisation.

It should be remembered that the reason for testing the perceptions of the rest of the organisation was to confirm or dispute the results yielded by the executive group.

The focus of the subsequent team coaching was to identify and discuss the main differences in opinion held by members of the executive team relating to the current versus the preferred culture. This part of the research process was about reaching Miletone 5, namely coaching for improved leadership practice or introducing steps to get everyone to understand the behavioural indicators of the preferred culture, since it became clear how members on lower organisational levels perceived the organisation's preferred culture.

Comparison: Survey results of the executive team and representative group

A comparison between executive team scores and representative group scores is given below.

The **power culture** was seen by both groups as of average strength, with both expressing a strong desire to diminish its power even more. Their results show remarkable similarity with regard to both the current and preferred **role culture**. Both teams saw this orientation as having average to strong influence in the organisation, and wanted to keep it as such.

With regard to the **achievement culture**, the representative group reflected almost the same scores as the executive team, with both realising its current strength and both wanting it to be even stronger. Lastly, both groups saw the need for the **support culture** to grow from average to strong.

In summary, the **achievement culture** was the most desired, followed by the **support culture** and the **role culture**, with the **power culture** being the least preferred. The results also served to demonstrate that the views held by the executive team were shared to a high degree by the rest of the organisation.

The next step was to probe the relevance and viability of the results of the organisational Survey with the full executive team to gain better insight into their personal perceptions of their organisational culture. A summary of perceptions gathered through meaningful coaching conversations is given in the following section.

Establishing the main issues of agreement

When I asked the executive team for their views on the causes of varying perceptions of organisational culture, they thought that differences in team members' roles and responsibilities resulted from varying backgrounds and differences in expectations.

My question to the executives was: "Which of the similarities between existing and preferred scores were significant?" Most of the executive team members reported that they were satisfied with the similarities in how the strengths of the cultures scored. This was seen as a decisive factor in reaching agreement about the culture or combination of cultures that was most preferred by the members of this executive team.

The high achievement orientation was seen to be positive in view of the project-driven nature of the organisation, which operated in a tough market where profit margins were negotiated to a minimum. The converse question, focusing on the disadvantages of the current combination of organisational cultures, produced the following responses:

- We may be too role-oriented to allow for growth in an achievement culture, which means that we may be so caught up in our designated roles and job descriptions that we hesitate, and even disallow others, to break the boundaries or even test them.
- There seems to be too little support for one another and our staff in this organisation.
- The leader's view is very different from the views of the rest of his team.
- Too much power is held by the two senior executives.

When asked which cultural influence should be reduced in the future, the response was that the general role orientation was too strong at present and needed to be played down. The majority of team members wanted to do away with this role orientation in the organisation. Instead, they felt there was a need to clarify job responsibilities for performance purposes.

Upon enquiring about the barriers that could hinder the client moving from its current reality to where it would like to be in terms of organisational culture, the main concerns were:

- the possibility that members may feel unsafe with fewer procedures, rules and guidelines (a diminishing role culture)
- the need for a safety net in the form of strengthened competence on all levels to empower people and, in so doing, to allow for mistakes (a characteristic of an achievement culture)
- the need to decide what exactly needs changing when it comes to leadership behaviours and indicators

My penultimate question related to the perceived potential of the movement towards a preferred culture to integrate the various business units of the organisation. The responses were positive, reflecting the need to marry the aims of the overall business with those of the various business units.

The last question I raised was: "What would be different in your organisation if the existing combination of cultures were to shift towards the preferred combination of cultures?" Most respondents claimed the differences would be better cooperation, more open relationships, better communication and increased business activity across business unit borders in order to strengthen the team. It was also felt that the organisation would have better direction and a better working atmosphere to attract more customers in the longer term, and would become a preferred company to work for.

The contributions indicated a strong need to agree on a desired culture that was viable and business-wise, and that would bring personal meaning to their working lives.

 Milestone 4: Determining variances between old and new cultures

This milestone set out to define a list of personal and team behaviours that would reflect the preferred culture within the organisation. The steps taken to get to this point were:

- Step 1: Identify the most significant variances between the current and preferred organisational cultures.
- Step 2: Agree on the critical leadership practices that constitute the preferred culture.

Step 1: Identify the most significant variances

Having reached clarity on their perceptions of the organisational culture, the executive team drew up an Excel spreadsheet that highlighted areas of significant variances between the current and preferred cultures as highlighted by the questionnaire. This matrix detailed the leadership practices that needed to change. In table 7.1, the left-hand column represents current leadership practices or behaviours that needed to change to become those of the desired culture, represented in the right-hand column.

Table 7.1: Significant variances between current and preferred cultures, as seen by the executive team

Current culture element	Preferred culture element
staying within the policies and procedures relating to jobs	meeting the challenges of the task, finding better ways of doing things
treating individuals like numbers	treating team members as peers, all mutually committed to achieving a common purpose
directives coming down from higher levels	more decisions to be made at the point of service
assignment of jobs according to competence and experience	matching requirements of jobs with the interests of individuals, plus their need for growth and development
job motivation coming from a place of guilt (not wanting to embarrass their superiors) instead of personal self-esteem	a stronger focus on self-motivation, taking the initiative and challenging leaders
managers and leaders being decisive and strong	leaders to be more supportive, responsive and caring about the concerns of staff
job motivation driven by following the norm and a fear of punishment	stimulate stronger desires to achieve, create and motivate
intervention of leaders in personal conflicts	conflict to be discussed with the aim of reaching the best outcome for all involved
people are tempted to break rules and hide such actions	more open support for the re-evaluation of rules
empowerment focused on role identification and the use of the power attached to a position	role descriptions to be replaced by goals, linked to rewards/incentives
sharing of information limited to those in positions of power	empowerment of all employees through improved sharing of information relevant to decision-making responsibility
work executed in silos (business units) resulting in specialised and focused customer products and unhealthy competition among business units	motivation to be created to work across boundaries towards common goals (complete solutions) and higher levels of responsiveness to customer needs

Main aim achieved

At this point, the study had achieved its main aim, namely to get the executive team of Viking Enterprises to reach agreement on the preferred organisational culture. The team expressed a need to integrate preferred leadership behaviours into the key areas most needing attention, such as communication, managing information and managing people.

In summary, the team wanted to reach agreement on those practices that would constitute the essence of the preferred culture (Milestone 4). Thereafter, individual coaching would probe the feasibility of developing the new practices in every member of the team (Milestone 5).

Step 2: Agree on critical leadership practices

During team coaching, the variances between current and preferred leadership practices were scrutinised and prioritised. Originally, 16 key areas were identified as factors with the potential to help the shift from the current towards the preferred culture. The team finally decided to work on 12 practices.

It was not yet clear how these practices should be exhibited in future. It was unanimously decided to use small teams to research the leadership practices necessary to reflect the preferred culture. Subsequent one-on-one coaching sessions would probe the development and usage of the preferred practices.

Milestone 5 achieved the outcomes of the small-team coaching aimed at addressing the 12 leadership issues prioritised above. The significant outcomes of the individual sessions gave every member of the team the opportunity to demonstrate willingness and resourcefulness to exchange current leadership behaviours for those new ones agreed by the team.

Milestone 5: Coaching for improved leadership practice

This milestone set out to define a list of personal and team behaviours that would reflect the preferred culture within the organisation. Gaining insight into team and individual perceptions of the new leadership practices enabled us to list the personal and team behaviours that would reflect the preferred organisational culture.

At this stage, only four months were left to complete the project. The executive team therefore decided to focus on three leadership practices per month of the 12 identified. Four rounds of team coaching were followed by small-group discussions and then by individual coaching for added impetus to make the deadline.

All the groups used the same format to report on their results. The agreed leadership practices, as they related to the issue at hand, were presented first, followed by the expected individual coaching outcomes. These related to the team members' perceptions of the viability of the new leadership behaviours.

The tabling of some of the issues received more attention than the reporting. The team had had time beforehand to actively enact the new behaviours, whereas reporting ceased after the 12th issue had been achieved. Effectively this meant that the agreement on reaching the leadership indicators and practices was exceeded, considering that much progress had been made with the actual practising of agreed leadership practices on most of the 12 issues.

The four rounds of team coaching produced various outcomes.

Round 1: Some coaching outcomes

A comprehensive sales strategy

Our team coaching reflections on sales strategy led to a detailed list of key leadership practices, which required greater attention to allow a diverse team of people with varied business interests to work closely together. Some of the more significant ones were:

- Strategies should be reduced to writing and should not be kept in the minds of those who formulated them.
- Decisions needed to be taken about who sells what and how sharing profit and loss would work.
- Guidelines needed to be formulated for marketing and selling efforts, and the sales reporting system should be used more optimally.
- The calendars of team members (all of whom had the responsibility for selling in their own businesses) were to be synchronised so that selling efforts could be combined and cross-selling opportunities could be leveraged.
- Sales processes needed to be defined and responsibility and authority levels in terms of sales needed to be clarified.

Most of the above points were accommodated in a comprehensive sales strategy, which evolved over the remaining time for the project. By that stage, every business unit leader and executive team member had committed to actions to promote his or her own business unit as well as to cross-sell the other units. The new situation indicated a significant shift from the silo effect that had characterised the culture up to that point.

Individual coaching feedback showed that the progress made with the collective sales strategy was pleasing, since it was the first constructive sign that people were willing and eager to do business together.

Contributions from the team members included the following:

- They had learnt that relationship building is very important and that they had much to learn about project selling.

- They felt good about their progress.
- The focus on new markets marked a stronger focus on achievement. The sales strategy led to team progress.
- The new sales presentation style and content was of great support to the salespeople.

In terms of attempts to strengthen the achievement culture, the person heading the sales strategy team reported improved cooperation between the various business units. Sales communications had been standardised. For example, the curricula vitae of all the consultants now served as a data bank to help decide which consultant to place with which customer. Logged reference projects gave sales personnel something to speak about when visiting new customers. All of these contributed to increased sales and profits.

Standardised communication also helped to ensure that team members worked towards the same goals and offered increased support to one another. The willingness of leaders to identify and log special competence areas among all staff promised to make them feel involved and recognised, and also supported customer needs.

Transparent and inclusive team decision-making

The following leadership practices were identified during team coaching as representative of the preferred culture:

- Levels of authority and responsibility for decision-making needed clarification, with a focus on empowerment. The key question related to those situations that warranted the core management team taking decisions unilaterally needed answering.
- Leaders had to be more open to having team members challenge their viewpoints.
- Leaders were to be less decisive and powerful. A greater focus on democracy and inclusion was necessary.
- Guidelines for conflict management were required.

The main issue upon which consensus was reached was the MD's commitment to share business issues, problems or opportunities with everyone, as and when they arose, using e-mail and inviting feedback and ideas. The MD would then take a decision together with the core management team, which comprised him and two other senior members of the executive team.

As time progressed, more workable guidelines were identified to guide the team with decision-making:

- Ensure that the number of issues to be decided upon is manageable.
- Distribute agendas at least 48 hours prior to meetings, indicating which discussions should take place at the meeting.
- Involve only those people impacted by the particular decision to be taken.
- Stick to dates set for meetings.
- Keep to the code of conduct.

The following individual perceptions of the team's progress with decision-making were shared:

- Yes, we are looking beyond our boxes to see what is good for the team and the company and we are developing a common way of thinking by strategising on the important decisions facing the team.
- The business judgement issue gives us up-to-date information regarding all sales activities and results. This brings about improved decision-making and leadership.

Sharing of information

Some team members reported that they did not get information first hand and had to hear about developments from others. Other employees felt ill-informed and isolated from the business. During team coaching the following leadership practices were agreed:

- The sharing of learning should receive more attention.
- Business information should be shared with consultants.
- People lower down should be better informed about the strategies and decisions taken at the top levels.

The outcomes following the implementation of the above decisions were:

- Teleconferencing was instituted on Monday afternoons to share opportunities for sales, new projects and the like.
- The MD shared business information with the entire executive team prior to sharing this information with the rest of the staff.
- Care was taken to send out clear information in a standardised way to all business units.
- Better communication systems were used to brief those consultants located in remote places.

Responses to the need to be more open included the following:

- Some positive growth is happening because members are given the opportunity to provide input for meeting agendas.
- We share all information openly with all team members now, with the understanding that we will not share it with them again if they leak it.

> **The phenomenological approach to team coaching**
>
> Through storytelling conversations, team members had much fun relating anecdotes from their personal lives, giving the rest of their team a better idea of what was meaningful to them. Shared stories emerged which reached beyond the **here and now** to **future** possibilities. Through this process, they co-created potential experiences with one another, representing a phenomenological development in the team.
>
> By reflecting upon the meaningfulness of the team coaching sessions, various team members reported significant progress. They took the trouble to explain their experiences of the session, based on their own interpretations, and found a number of the team coaching outcomes meaningful and of much value. As early as the first round, I saw that the application of phenomenological principles during team sessions contributed to the team's progress towards a preferred way of working together.

Round 2: Some coaching outcomes

Strategic alignment

In essence, this meant that the business plans of the six business units had to be integrated. It would be a bonus if, at the end of the process, the team realised the need to integrate the strategic goals of the company with the cultural outcomes under discussion.

Team coaching resulted in the team taking meaningful decisions. Firstly, a set of leadership practices was identified as a key area for development:

- Set common goals and communicate these to everyone involved.
- Make goals more challenging by linking measurements to them.
- Collectively (as the executive team) decide on priority issues and ensure that goals are measured.
- Management should set some goals, but some freedom should be left to the individuals tasked with the responsibility of achieving these goals.
- Review the current performance management strategy to provide for measurements and institute this as part and parcel of the new strategic drive within the organisation.

Firstly, the above strategy provided greater clarity on reporting lines and responsibilities. The new system provided individual staff members with greater motivation to achieve improved production and financial results.

Secondly, it was decided to combine the BSCs of the six business units into a single scorecard for the whole organisation (see figure 7.1).

Thirdly, the new company strategy was compared with a SWOT analysis undertaken by the team during the analysis part of the strategic process, prior to analysing their organisational culture.

Refer to the integrated BSC of Viking Enterprises in Appendix B.

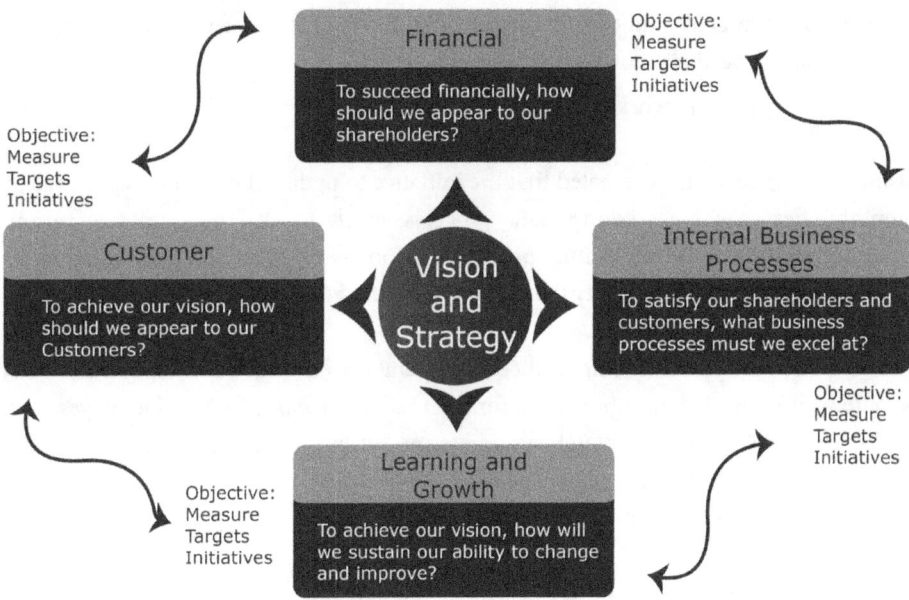

Figure 7.1: The balanced scorecard pro forma used by Viking Enterprises[69]

Individual coaching on progress combined with the fostering of the leadership practices led to comments such as:

- We are more aware of each other's businesses now.
- We have taken a couple of steps forward more quickly than we would have done without this process.
- We are more informed about where we stand with certain things.
- We now know each other's business and have one BSC for the company. This brings about transparency, awareness, better reaction time and therefore more achievement and support.

- The work of both the sales strategy and project evaluation subgroups has been incorporated into our management meetings. This means that we are starting to integrate culture with business.

Cooperation: Project- and consultancy-oriented business units

The rationale behind this move was to raise motivation across business unit boundaries to higher levels of responsiveness. The common sales strategy was an important first step towards setting common sales goals that involved both consultancy-oriented and project-oriented business units.

Leadership tasks to be addressed to facilitate the agreed preferred culture included:

- Set common goals and communicate them, allowing some leeway to challenge the rules and procedures currently in existence.
- Motivate people to work across business unit boundaries.

Team coaching reflections revealed that the initiative to update the original sales strategy monthly after coaching sessions made progress visible to all. The team saw various groupings of team members visiting potential customers together, and combining forces on new projects where previously they thought they had nothing in common.

With regard to the perceived importance of cooperation, one individual reported: "I don't want to work alone. Relationships work for me; that's what works for me, and oh yes, trust works for me too!" Another member came to me because he thought that he may have been a threat to some team members because of his bold selling approach. He undertook to be more inclusive in his quest for new business.

Once better cooperation had been established, the outcomes reflected an overall positive expectation of both a stronger sense of achievement and stronger support across business unit boundaries. Managers made comments such as:

- The special competence areas discovered among some staff members make them feel useful and recognised, and support customers and enhance our own business competence.
- We are more aware than before of how we should work together, although we may need some action steps like the ones in the sales and project work teams.
- We are starting to sell each other's business, and need to focus on this aspect much more.

A strategy for project management

During the team coaching session, it was decided to task one person with the responsibility for developing a project management system. The team had to assist him with input, test runs and feedback. The person chosen to develop this system was highly regarded and trusted by all. During a team brainstorming session the following key points were listed as being useful to consider in the development of this system:

- The checklist in use at the time should be applied to calculate risk and to ensure that all questions with regard to a new project are answered. This tool supported decisions to quote or not to quote.
- A best-practice guidelines document for the management of projects was commissioned, including a software program that interfaced with the reporting systems of the organisation.
- Best-practice policies and guidelines should be developed and incorporated into project training workshops.
- The system/program should be able to do quality checks on cost calculations.

During the individual coaching sessions, the team members' perceptions confirmed positive shifts in role clarity, improved control, a sense of achievement and increased support for the project management system. Those who used the system felt it was making a strong contribution towards the development of the preferred organisational culture.

Round 3: Some coaching outcomes

More attention to people management

The team decided that this leadership issue needed to be addressed in the one-on-one coaching sessions due to its sensitive nature. This issue linked closely with the need for a revised performance management system and for strategic alignment.

Once strategic and cultural alignment was achieved with performance measurement agreed by the executive team, every business unit manager introduced staff members to the new vision, the BSCs of the company and divisional units, together with the improved performance management system.

During the individual coaching sessions, the team members were asked which combination of cultures they believed would foster better people management. All agreed that the following key people management practices would foster the preferred cultures:

- Before we did the cultural training day, I could see the power and support cultures, but did not know what was in the middle of that.
- Before this session, I thought that support would be best, and only support culture because my view was that you should have team building without having to tell people what they should do.
- I try to increase their responsibility and authority. I view all of these things as part of my supportive role as a manager.

The youngest member of the team reported that he would know that his team members supported and valued each other when he was able to phone them as peers to ask for their guidance.

They all indicted a strong need to be recognised for their contributions to the team and to the organisation.

Better-managed meetings

At the outset of this research project, which kicked off with team coaching sessions, it was decided that the team needed to develop an organisational strategy before they could decide on a new culture.

When it came to deliberating this issue and the necessary leadership behaviours for effective meetings, it was decided to adopt the existing company code of conduct as the mandatory guideline for future meetings. It had been in practice for a number of team meetings and seemed to have a positive effect.

The code of conduct accepted by the executive team is included at the back of this book as Appendix C.

Individual member reflections: improvements

Comments by staff members on improvements made during the period of setting the milestones included:

- Improvements now reflect a better focus because discussions are divided into sales, projects, information and decisions. This reduces the frustration at meetings.
- New telephone meetings on Mondays instituted by the leader of this group are working well.
- We know what is happening in all business units; it is informative and supportive.

Round 4: Some coaching outcomes

The way in which performance is measured in the organisation should facilitate cooperation between project and consultancy.

The executive team decided to bring in a consultant to do some performance management training for the team. Keeping in mind that the team saw a combination of achievement and support as their preferred cultural orientation, a key factor was the extent to which the training would facilitate constructive conversations around these two key leadership orientations.

The first training module focused on the strategic importance of measuring and managing performance. Key learning revolved around the type of messages leaders sent out into the company, particularly in the way that they managed the performance of their teams. The executive team explored questions about their current performance measurement form, and discovered that it allowed for perhaps too much subjectivity on the part of the leader and also tended to measure aspects unrelated to performance.

They made an informed decision that the performance measurements should reflect the new way of leading and measuring. This decision led to the reconstruction of the performance measurement form. It also changed their perceptions of the roles they should be playing to ensure that performance management did lead to enhanced achievement.

The second training module focused on implementing and practising better performance management as a key leadership competence. It stressed the importance of being supportive in terms of developing individuals and creating a supportive cultural orientation.

The next step was to critically evaluate the current way of planning and monitoring performance against the principles learnt, and to enhance the process. They decided against making radical changes to the performance measurement system, as that would create unnecessary resistance to change. It was agreed that the performance measurement forms needed to be easy to understand and that managers should view the system as a management tool and not as unnecessary paperwork.

The new performance measurement form is given at the back of the book as Appendix D.

Development in competence

The team realised that it could be putting the cart before the horse to finalise a competence development plan before the new strategy and culture were rolled out in the organisation. Hence, they decided to focus only on project management competence. They would do a complete competence needs analysis once all performance planning and development talks were finalised and they had a clear picture of the competence developmental needs of the organisation.

A project trainer was sourced and by the end of this research project, 27 members of the organisation had been trained in project management. The next step was to get them working as a group to develop best-practice policies and guidelines that incorporated the new learning.

The above best-practice guidelines in project management had to feature in the system being designed to manage and monitor project results. The outcome of this cannot be given here, since it represents a crucial part of the competitive advantage of the client organisation in the field of project management. All the feedback received during one-on-one coaching sessions indicated that the envisaged system, coupled with the newly acquired project management competence, significantly increased the achievement potential of the organisation.

An induction programme

In the absence of an HR function, the team decided that every business unit manager would be responsible for the induction of new staff members in their business units. The team agreed that the current induction programme offered substantial information and material to every business unit manager to help him or her orient new staff members entering the organisation. The induction programme included explaining the company name, new vision and strategy, business unit strategies, sales strategy, a performance and development planning system and a project reporting system.

At the final team coaching session, which also served to wrap up the entire process, a checklist was completed which measured how the original issues had been addressed. It was clear that more progress had been made on some of the issues addressed earlier, and less on those addressed later in the process. The reason was that the agreements instituted earlier gave team members more time to practise the agreed behaviours relating to these issues. The team nevertheless agreed that enough progress had been made in total, and committed themselves to continued growth and development in all agreed leadership practices.

The final milestone for purposes of reporting on the results of this research project was the pursuit of leadership practices that would facilitate the company's preferred culture.

 ## Milestone 6: Setting goals to facilitate the preferred culture

This milestone aimed to develop a set of personal practices and a set of leadership practices that would facilitate growth towards the development of the preferred culture.

Through the team coaching sessions, agreement was reached on the developmental activities that the executive team should undertake in order to ensure the facilitation of the preferred culture. During these sessions, priority areas were identified and brainstormed, and plans were formulated for the development of the envisaged new culture.

The one-on-one coaching sessions after the team coaching sessions were aimed at probing the feasibility of enhancing those leadership practices representative of the preferred culture. Individual leaders had to decide which behaviours they felt they wanted to address in terms of leading their own team of people. Individual plans took the form of BSCs for each leader's business unit, and integrated well with the strategic direction decided upon for the organisation.

Using the BSC to represent the cultural alignment goals was more than I could have hoped for. This effectively meant that team members grasped the link between strategy and culture, and were willing to indicate their commitment to the preferred culture alongside their strategic goals on one BSC for all to see.

The following commitments were made with regard to how customers should be managed once the new culture was adopted:

- Apply ISO tools to generate customer feedback. ISO refers to the standards of the International Organization for Standardization, to which international businesses must conform to prove their commitment and ability to deliver work that meets international quality standards.
- Use high standards such as those of ISO to provide an indication of how role orientation should be tightened up by adhering to set norms and standards. This goal also reflects a strong achievement orientation, in that compliance with international standards immediately opens up business opportunities.
- Provide ongoing feedback on customer satisfaction to all staff to facilitate growth and improvement. This commitment would serve to inform staff of customer satisfaction levels and support them with important information upon which to base business improvement decisions.
- Provide optimum service by offering the most appropriate competence available. This commitment aimed for better fulfilment of customer needs to enhance the image of the organisation as perceived by its customers.
- Keep all staff updated on customer needs and feedback. This action would gear staff for better service delivery, which the customers reportedly wanted.
- Encourage staff to build and maintain a customer network. This would provide a supportive network and also improve communication and cooperation among the various business units of the organisation.

In summary, the following commitments were made in terms of the cultural indicators to smarten up business processes in the organisation:

- Make leadership involvement a requirement when deciding on the strategic viability of all potential projects. This leadership must focus less on power and more on support.
- Use leadership to ensure optimal results in all projects. This calls for stronger support and clearly defined leadership roles.
- Provide leadership support to establish teamwork and a sense of pride and belonging.
- Leverage cross-selling opportunities that can foster closer working relations between various business units, strengthening both achievement and support orientations.
- Stimulate better cooperation among various business units through a focused approach to using our total competence, which again represents both of the preferred cultures, namely achievement and support.

Finally, these commitments were made to develop people:

- Agree on competence developmental goals for every staff member, which will strengthen the achievement potential of each employee.
- Stimulate employees to explore new challenges (work in different areas) and to expand their roles based on their interests.
- Develop a culture that fosters achievement by ensuring individual goal-setting and motivation.
- Encourage each employee, through engagement, to plan proactively for future business and to acquire the competencies needed to achieve success.
- Provide a learning environment by sharing lessons learnt and by considering employees' personal interests and circumstances when placing them in new jobs.

The BSCs of both the business units and the organisation reflected goals that:

- fostered the preferred combination of cultures, which meant less power
- focused on the identification and clarification of more appropriate roles
- rejected a stronger role orientation per se
- preferred a very strong achievement culture in combination with a strong supportive culture

CONCLUSION

The project process described in this chapter is made up of steps within milestones. The outcomes of all the milestones were reached and the process of facilitating agreement among all the members of an executive team regarding the preferred culture was successfully concluded.

If I had used the force field analysis tool for the process described above, it would have looked something like figure 7.2 (as seen through my eyes):

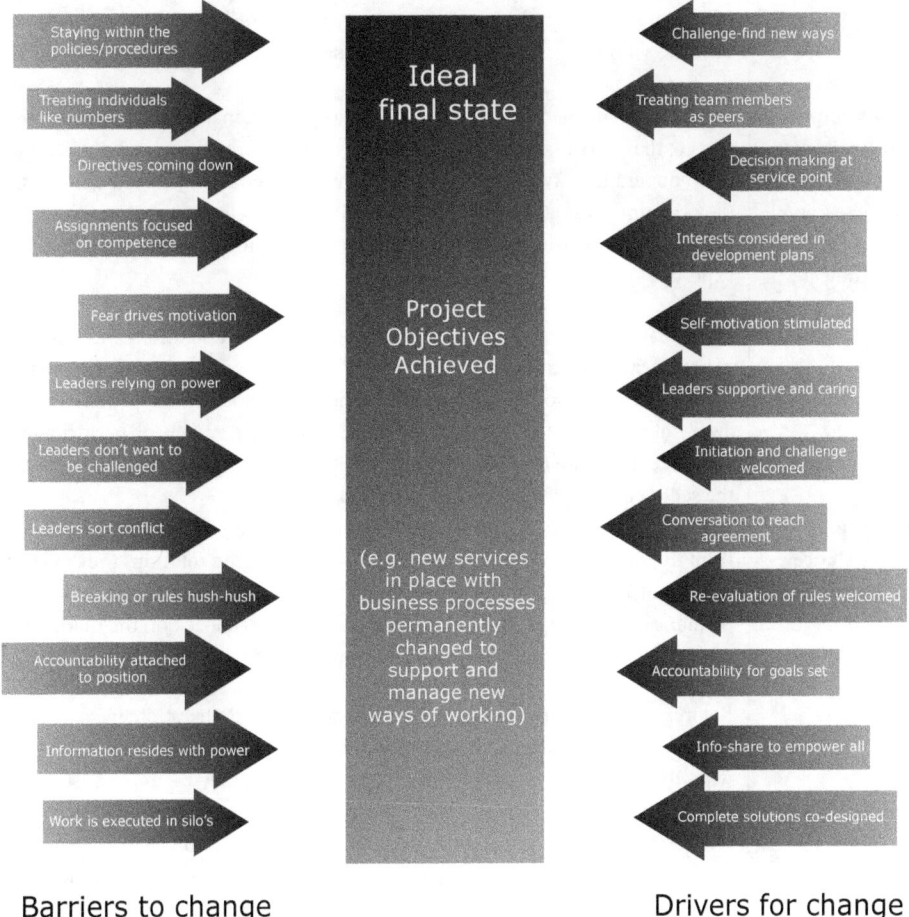

Figure 7.2: Force field analysis of Viking Enterprises after setting milestones and reaching agreement

In chapter 3, I mentioned that my coaching is greatly informed by the four-stage conscious competence theory. I present my interpretation of the learning that happened among the Viking team members as the process described in this chapter unfolded:

Table 7.2: Four stages of the conscious competence theory, with examples of behaviours displayed by the executive team of Viking Enterprises during each stage

Stage	Example of actual behaviour at each stage in the coaching process at Viking Enterprises
Unconscious incompetence (members do not know "that they do not know")	Six executive team members represented their own divisions and three represented the head office. When I met them, the members were experiencing a lack of communication and cooperation (and other things) among themselves. They did not know the reasons for this state of disharmony.

Marketing costs were high as clients were not routinely returning to do more business with them. The reasons for this situation were unclear at that stage of the process. |
| **Conscious incompetence** (members come to know "that they do not know") | Once the team members completed the organisational culture survey, they agreed that two of their main challenges (as a team) were communication and cooperation. When they eventually considered their daily work habits, they became aware that they were not selling complete engineering solutions. Instead, each division followed a silo approach, focusing only on its own expertise.

Up to that point, they all believed that offering complete solutions was not part of how they did business and they were therefore not required to take along the heads of any of the other divisions when visiting customers. They then became aware of the need to do so, and accepted that their system of performance incentives based on individual leadership effort did not promote teamwork and the selling of complete engineering solutions. |
| **Conscious competence** (members do something "to get to know") | At the early team coaching sessions, executive members agreed to get feedback from their clients about the relevance of the engineering solutions they offered and about their current service standards. Having done so, members started regular sales meetings where they shared customer feedback on the marketing of complete solutions instead of just offering their unique specialities.

Before meeting with customers, members discussed the strategy to follow. Then, unusually for them, they met customers together. Afterwards, they shared what they had learnt from the meetings. Therefore, they became consciously (knowingly) skilled at better internal communication and cooperation, while offering new services and solutions based on customer feedback. |
| **Unconscious competence** (members forget "that they now know" and they display new behaviour instinctively) | The team was pleasantly surprised to discover that the annual sales conference produced figures showing that sales of total solutions outperformed those for single, specialised products and processes, and did so by far. They also received customer feedback indicating a sense of strong cooperation from senior company representatives.

Their collective sales efforts produced much better teamwork and cooperation, as they were compelled to be more open in their communications with one another. |

Chapter 8

SUCCESS FOR VIKING ENTERPRISES!

Just how much progress has Viking Enterprises made with regard to the actual establishment of their preferred culture? What kinds of things happened along the way? Well, let's see.

In the South African winter of 2010 I had a surprise phone call from Per, the 2IC with whom I had worked at Viking Enterprises. Per told me that the company had significantly scaled down operations in order to work towards a culture of high performance and support. Viking Enterprises had found its niche, which was specialisation in the core business of engineering projects and robotics, with Per as MD. Nielsen Gerhrke, the former MD, had moved on to start his own company. Nielsen had always had a knack for commercial property development and was pursuing his interest in this field.

Per said that Viking Enterprises had had its best financial year since the introduction of the coaching intervention. He was very sure that the upturn was a result of their focus on their preferred culture and leadership practices, and how this translated into daily routines meant to sustain their efforts. I was delighted by this news. Per wanted me to do a follow-up survey to determine to what extent their culture had indeed shifted from a control- and role-oriented culture to one characterised by performance and support.

I was intrigued! I asked how they were doing. According to Per, only four of the original nine executive team members were still part of the organisation. Some had left for better job opportunities, while others just did not enjoy the focus on performance through better cooperation and felt that they did not fit in any more.

The company had shifted its focus and improved its internal cooperation to maximise outputs, mainly through increased economies of scale. In fact, they were doing so well at the time of Per's call that they had two industry bidders wanting to buy them out. Per said they would definitely sell at the right price! "This is all very well and very interesting", I said to Per, "but what do you really think brought the company to this point?" He responded: "Undoubtedly, it was the decision we took to implement our preferred organisational culture as well as our continual efforts to entrench it in our daily practices."

Viking Enterprises now has "preferred culture" on the agenda of every meeting and staff keep each other accountable through the BSCs. Per said in his determined way: "Salomé, I do know that what we did worked. We are now truly performance-driven; we make good margins and our team acts as one and we all support one another. We are so proud of having achieved a turnaround in the company."

My conversation with Per ended with arrangements for me to visit Sweden once again to use the Harrison and Stokes questionnaire as a postproject measurement instrument at Viking Enterprises.

Was this telephone call from Per not a revelation? How many practitioners are given this opportunity to draw inspiration from clients who have successfully implemented and sustained a project of this nature? I felt utterly blessed!

During September 2010, I conducted a follow-up study at Viking Enterprises. The survey instrument of Harrison and Stokes was used again at the now smaller Viking Enterprises (Projects and Robotics) and the following clear cultural shifts were noted:

- Viking Enterprises had made the transition from the unwanted control and role-orientated culture to the planned performance-driven and support-orientated culture.
- They had achieved all the goals they had set at the end of the original project.

What delightful news! Even more pleasing was the qualitative feedback I received about the leadership practices they had sought to embrace. These are some of the things I was told, shown in table 8.1:

Table 8.1: Sheet of achievements

Required changes in the culture of Viking Enterprises as seen by the leaders, moving from a control and role orientation to an environment characterised by achievement and support	
Current culture (previously)	*Achievement and explanation of achievement*
Develop a comprehensive company strategy and align everyone accordingly (common goals).	We have a strategy and it has been achieved. Our sales director shares the overall mission with everyone during performance discussions. Still to do: New goals need to be set for our working strategy over the medium term.

Required changes in the culture of Viking Enterprises as seen by the leaders, moving from a control and role orientation to an environment characterised by achievement and support	
Current culture (previously)	*Achievement and explanation of achievement*
Practise more inclusive and more transparent decision-making.	Decision-making has shifted down to director level. They work as a team on a daily basis and are now much more transparent. To continue doing: The focus of control is still centred at directorate level to ensure that decisions are inclusive, and as close to the operations as possible.
Facilitate better cooperation between different parts of the business (eg consultancy and projects).	Since the business is now much more focused, we have the flexibility to add new business to our portfolio where we have the expertise and capacity to do so. To be aware of: Our offering is now much more exclusive. We need to be careful not to be seen as elitist.
Design and implement a proper project management strategy, system and processes.	We have done this and are continually assessing and incorporating new technology, processes and routines to stay at the leading edge. Still to achieve: Project management is there for financial control reasons mostly and is not used by all project leaders. Some still need to be educated to do so.
Invest in an improved company image and increased public awareness.	Branding is much stronger today than before. Our clients have confidence and trust in our ability to deliver. We have made excellent progress, but we need to stay humble.
Practise better people management.	This is a real strength now, although this is the perception of the leaders. It would make good to sense to find out how the associates feel about management.
Manage meetings better (time, openness, one agenda and all-round participation).	Things are much better now that we are all in one location. We keep each other on our toes with regard to time and follow-through. However, there is no clear measurement of how well we are doing this. We just track the cost of time spent on meetings, but have to re-evaluate this in order to determine the need for further growth in this area.

Required changes in the culture of Viking Enterprises as seen by the leaders, moving from a control and role orientation to an environment characterised by achievement and support	
Current culture (previously)	*Achievement and explanation of achievement*
Develop and implement better performance management. Focus on measurable targets/goals.	Salaries are now based on personal expertise and experience. Incentives are based on a project team basis.
Develop competence in core business skills such as project management.	Yes, we are developing people – critical but difficult. What could have been done/can still be done? We should have done more succession planning and mentorship. We lost some key people by not doing this. We need to get this going.

In short, Viking Enterprises had been reshaped and rebranded. It is much smaller and more focused and it offers customers only that which it can deliver successfully. The organisation has achieved a major shift in culture and is now more performance-driven and supportive. In essence Viking Enterprises offers total solutions, with customers coming back for more on account of good project delivery. This really was their main aim with the coaching project. You may want to know if they have sold the company. The answer is YES!

Table 8.1 indicates that there is more work to be done, and, thank goodness, they don't think that they have arrived yet!

Having rolled out the process distilled through my work in Sweden, I have subsequently discovered that the Viking Enterprises process is flexible enough to accommodate a variety of contexts and challenges, particularly in Africa. I share more about this with you in the next chapter.

Chapter 9

ADAPTING THE COACHING PROCESS TO ACHIEVE ALIGNMENT IN VARIOUS CONTEXTS

INTRODUCTION

In this chapter I share with you how I have adapted the team alignment process described in chapter 6 to meet the needs of client organisations in contexts different to that of Viking Enterprises. To do this, I first had to decide on the applicability of the milestones. Some clients required the whole "Viking Enterprises process", while others only needed a part of it.

I found the process I had originally devised very flexible. As the needs of clients, and even their status quo, differ, the style of coaching has to be adapted. Thus, new milestones are added while others must be shifted or swopped to reach the various objectives.

The two case studies below illustrate how you as a coach can make this team alignment process your own.

CASE STUDY 1

An international logistics company in a neighbouring country required coaching for its HR team to ensure better service delivery to the functional areas of the business. I was invited to visit this company for a week to be briefed, assess the situation and decide whether or not I wanted to engage with them, and they with me.

After receiving my brief from the MD, I asked for time with the HR team, individually and as a group, to understand their perceptions. These included HR needs expressed by line management, the responsiveness of HR and any HR team dynamics. I also attended the monthly management meeting to get a sense of how the HR manager interacted with his peers. Through observation in this setting and especially by judging body language, I realised that the HR manager did not have much authority in the management meeting. He was almost considered a second-class citizen, if I can be this blunt. However, in his own HR team of four staff members he had more authority and used the strengths of his individual team members quite well.

The HR manager's management style was business-oriented. Yet I noticed little evidence of team cohesion. His empowerment style was close to abdication; he was clearly under stress and had a poor self-image. In short, my summary of my first fact-finding week was that the HR manager was not perceived to have influence in the management team. He was often treated in a dismissive manner, while the work of his team was criticised as lacking innovation, relevance and service orientation. Also, the entire team was generally weak in building relationships with the functional managers.

It dawned on me that more work needed to be done than the MD had anticipated.

After spending a week with the client organisation and obtaining a commitment (and contract) from them to offer coaching to the HR team and HR manager, I flew back to Cape Town and used my thoughts and reflections to create the best process of coaching that would work for my client.

It became clear to me that I lacked a way to measure effectiveness at the end of my work with the HR team of the organisation. In follow-up Skype sessions with the HR manager and later with the MD, I asked both of them the same question: "For the coaching intervention to be perceived as successful, what needs to be in place and to be different, absent or better?"

The HR manager said that he wanted to feel a legitimate part of the management team and not like a second-class citizen. He wanted to develop more self-confidence so that peers would take his professional advice to heart and, most of all, he wanted a better relationship with his team and peers (line functionaries), in that order. The MD, however, wanted better service from the HR team and better performance from the man heading the team. The MD felt that he often had to step in and handle difficult matters on their behalf, such as negotiating with the unions.

To cut a long story short, I spent one week, from Monday to Friday, every month with the organisation, and I did this for a year. During this time I worked closely with the team, assessing both their individual and collective personalities, strengths, development needs and innermost desires for personal and career development, as well as their goals for growth – as individuals and as a team.

My coaching weeks involved meeting the HR manager away from the office on a Monday afternoon. I then coached him for at least two hours. That gave me the opportunity to assess his state of mind, capacity, energy and mood, but also to hear his side of "how business is going with regard to his team serving the line". Then we prepared for the following week. We also set up one-on-one coaching sessions for his team members and a team session on the Friday morning before I left the country.

In between these commitments I spent time summarising, reflecting on and integrating my new-found knowledge and set up meetings with others in the organisation to brainstorm and ask for feedback and the like. Whenever management meetings were held with market-sensitive information as part of the agenda, I was required to leave the room.

So, which of the milestones from Viking Enterprises were used in this African project?

Milestone 1: Finding the real "shared concern"

It took me the whole of the first week to determine the real concerns. I must admit I learnt even more along the way during the following three months. I realised again that I needed to be careful not to set objectives too early in the process. Only after clients have truly learnt to trust me will they will share "real issues" with me.

The reflective power of coaching also stimulates issues to rise from the subconscious to the conscious mind, and often clients realise true bugbears and things that make them happy only through the "look in the mirror" and the safe space that we as coaches provide. Now, I tell my clients that at best, the original goals set for such processes may be only a good guess. I caution them that these milestones may take a different shape or even shift through the process of coaching.

Milestone 2: Reaching agreement on the process (way of working) and the goals to be reached

It took me a week to discover the rhythm of the client organisation, and I am thankful that I was given this time to discover and distil the inter-relationships, expectations and atmosphere of the organisation. I am also very grateful for the almost blunt honesty coming from both the MD and the HR manager.

I have described my weekly "routine" to you, not that I like routine, but I find that this is useful for the stakeholders in the client organisation. When you are given the freedom to attend management meetings and meet whomever you deem appropriate in order to do your work, take care not to abuse it. In fact you should respect and treasure that arrangement, as it provides a platform for mutual trust.

Milestone 3: Sharing perceptions and reflecting upon behaviours to meet the set goals

This milestone was very relevant throughout the process. Of course, it was important to discover as soon as possible what people thought were the behaviours and thinking that might hamper achieving the desired outcomes. Of equal importance was keeping an open mind on possible shifts in perception, together with unlearning old behaviours and habits and practising new ones.

Milestone 4: Determining variances between current and preferred "ways of being and doing"

This milestone was an ongoing one and very relevant throughout the intervention. Yet, quite soon in the process, the HR team and its manager realised that they had to perform better by doing (among other things) the following:

- Increase their service levels to the line or functional managers.
- Build relationships with line or functional managers.
- Find solutions that work for the organisation and sell these to all staff, or help line managers to sell them to staff.
- Follow up and stick with a situation until it is resolved.
- Find their voices and build their confidence in order to use their influence.
- Speak up when they did not have access to resources, especially sources of information.

Milestone 5: Coaching for priority behavioural issues or leadership practice, according to individual and collective goals of all stakeholders

Every coaching session focused on the particular goals of the individual or the team with regard to different ways of thinking, being or doing. Slowly, individuals found their voices, learnt to assert themselves, armed themselves with goodwill, developed ample resilience and found workable solutions.

What became evident from this case study is that the milestones of the original process had to be rewritten and shifted to suit the needs of a client from a very different industry and a very different culture to that of Viking Enterprises. Yet the core milestones remained the same. The project approach to managing the process was retained and milestones were tracked on a continual basis, after which the MD received feedback on progress, with a full report from me at the end of the project.

CASE STUDY 2

Background

After having spent years in the field of training and facilitation, I realised that training often brings about a short-lived feeling of curiosity, with attempts to implement some of the new learning. The implementation of new knowledge and skills often falls flat soon afterwards because either the stakeholders in the learners' immediate environment do not support it, or the learner does not feel empowered enough to carry it through.

The current economic climate creates a high demand for learning and development processes that cost less money and involve less travel. The challenge for providers of learning is to find relevant metrics to prove that their offering makes economic sense. Online learning platforms and blended learning approaches are becoming increasingly popular. They are readily accessible, affordable (and in many instances free) and are often more captivating to learners than traditional classroom learning. It is also imperative to link learning metrics with learning outcomes, since this approach resonates with those people who have influence over budgets. Learning interventions that promise a return on investment, even a return on learning investment (ROLI), are being considered more often.

Changes in behaviour and performance after training and coaching will not be immediate, but are likely to show once new learning has been implemented, with time allowed for the impact of the changes to appear. Impact may be experienced in ways such as shorter delivery times, saved costs, improved relationships and higher sales.

In this case study, a period of training was followed by a coaching intervention to ensure better and faster learning transfer to the workplace, as well as more sustainable project management practices.

How the case study started

In 2008, a petroleum organisation approached me, asking if I would help with the development of project management capacity within one of its divisions where it was losing money due to poor project management. They seemed to have done extensive training in project management over many years, but struggled to make a positive impact on the bottom line. Projects took much longer than originally expected, or exceeded budget allocations. Their margin slippage became a real concern.

In an effort to find best practice, they sent various people on a variety of project management programmes in the hope that they would come back and make a difference. Instead, what they achieved was chaos, with managers using different terms and software to manage their projects. There was almost a sense of "one-upmanship" with regard to the project methodology employed.

It was important from the outset of the case study to unearth all perceptions about the state of affairs in projects, to define the desired scenario and to understand how progress would be measured. The challenge then would be to find a workable solution from a range of viable and relevant development approaches, and finally to achieve implementation.

Milestones

The following five milestones were developed:

Milestone 1: To ascertain the project management methodology and measurement of results used in the relevant business division during the previous financial year

At first, the execution of this milestone seemed more troublesome than expected because the organisation did not have an institutionally agreed way of comparing the success of one project with another. Apart from recording financial margins and time, very little was done to capture the possible causes of delay. What complicated the matter even more was that the project managers had all learnt from different schools of project knowledge.

Milestone 2: To determine the preferred project management methodology and measurement of results in the relevant business unit responsible for the successful implementation of projects

After a long and difficult debate, it was agreed that the organisation would re-institute its own training in project management and project leadership and, with the help of all the project managers, adapt and review the course content. This was a significant accomplishment for the division and it provided inclusivity in the project, which was one of the keys to success.

The best part of this feedback was that newly learnt skills needed to be practised immediately with the help of on-the-job "hand-holding". As I mentioned earlier in this book, my involvement in assessment centres has taught me that feedback, followed up with coaching, allows for greater transference of knowledge and skills than feedback alone.

A valid question was raised: "How will we measure the impact of the coaching?" After more debate, it was decided that "return on investment" was not a viable measure for this project, and that "return on learning investment" would be a more realistic measure. A simple formula was designed to place the costs of the exercise of training and coaching on the "debit side" and to weigh them up against increased performance by the relevant department over a one-year period. On the "credit side" of the equation, the financial implications of the following performance indicators were considered:

- lower margin slippage
- more projects being delivered on or before the planned date of completion
- less time spent in meetings
- lower cost of industrial action
- lower turnover of staff on projects due to increased levels of motivation

Milestone 3: To train all project managers in the preferred way of planning, executing, managing and measuring projects

Milestone 4: To offer on-the-job coaching to all managers once they had received training, enabling them to apply their new-found learning without delay

> **Milestone 5: To ascertain if the preferred way of managing projects produced results different to those of the previous way of managing projects**
>
> Learners/coachees reported tremendous progress in their ability to influence others because of a stronger personal conviction that their contribution was appropriate and relevant.
>
> The skill of reflection, harnessed through coaching, helped them to internalise learning faster and more confidently. Their stronger performance on their respective projects and their improved relationships with stakeholders made them feel that they had careers and not just jobs. Besides these qualitative results, many reported time and cost savings on projects due to improved responsiveness, confidence, insight and assertiveness.
>
> Line managers reported that enhanced learning, strengthened by coaching, facilitated newly trained project managers to take more responsibility for their actions. This, in turn, resulted in a stronger action orientation and better problem-solving. All of the above contributed to more timely delivery and reduced margin slippage on projects led by learners who had been part of this pilot study. Some reported better relationships with learners, while most concluded that coaching had added value to the business.
>
> Sponsors of the project embraced the approach used in the case study. It contributed to overall company performance, aside from the measurement of ROLI. Sponsors were also swayed by the higher levels of competent project leadership in the division concerned.

My own learning

This project taught me that ROLI is higher when:

- The newly acquired competence is viable for the company or business, relevant to the job at hand and personally meaningful to the learner in that it facilitates higher performance.
- Transfer of learning to the workplace is welcomed and/or facilitated by the leader or manager of the work unit, especially when he or she understands and believes that the new learning can lead to better performance.
- There is an immediate need for implementation of the newly learnt knowledge or skill in the form of a work-based assignment or project aimed at improving the status quo.

- The newly trained individual feels empowered to try out his or her new learning (feels trusted, able and motivated).

The question may be asked: "What contribution did coaching make to enhancing the above conditions for improved ROLI in this case study?" Well, coaching was aimed at strategically defined and job-specific competences of project management. Both the training and the coaching were thus relevant and personally meaningful.

The transfer of learning to the workplace was facilitated by:

- involving the line manager in the process, training him on the process and explaining the possible benefits to him
- using pre- and postprocess questionnaires about the contribution made by the new learning
- training the coaches, who came from a project management background, in the company's preferred way of managing projects
- enhancing the immediacy of implementation, because every learner was managing his or her own real-life project, or was a team member on such a project
- improving learner readiness through coaching, which enabled learners to handle the challenges within their projects in a more empowered way. This readiness came about because learners' self-belief was strengthened, communication skills were improved and awareness was created of ways to constructively use their influence or secure the support and goodwill of those in key positions.

CONCLUDING COMMENTS

The message that I want to leave with you in this chapter is that a personally developed framework and/or model is important. As coaches, we can borrow all we want from others, but it is only once we have developed an approach true to ourselves (what we bring, how we do it and what we leave behind) that we are able to offer consistently good coaching. In so doing, we strengthen the image of coaching as a responsibility and a sustainable development practice.

Chapter 10

LEARNING AND REFLECTIONS ON ETHICS IN COACHING

INTRODUCTION

Threaded throughout this book are (covert) issues of ethics and confidentiality that I embrace as a practitioner of coaching, and for that matter, as a consultant and training facilitator. I think we should first find agreement on what is generally understood by the word "ethics" in the fields of professional coaching and mentoring in this country. After discussing the meaning of ethics, I share a few of the ethical challenges I have experienced over the years, and specifically with the implementation of the projects described in this book. Please appreciate that this is just a snapshot of my personal interpretation, learning and reflection on the subject.

WHAT ARE ETHICS?

As in any other discipline, the matter of ethical standards is paramount in the field of professional coaching. Here, the coach is deeply involved with human emotions and even psychological trauma. Matters of ethics and confidentiality should therefore be accorded high significance.

My personal belief about ethics is that it is a discipline that points to the need for people to hold the minimal values and priorities required to lead creative and productive lives (as opposed to destructive lives). Ethics are also important if people exert some degree of influence on others.

Whose ethics code to follow?

I subscribe to the ethical and professional standards of Comensa, a not-for-gain umbrella organisation that regulates ethical conduct for the coaching profession in this country. The mission of Comensa is to set ethical standards for practitioners in the fields of coaching and mentoring. Thus, the body sets up and upholds an appropriate code of ethics that defines the ethical behaviour supporting the expanding coaching profession.

Do I embrace the ethics of international coaching bodies? Most definately yes! When I engage in coaching in partnership with valued associates from the Global Coach Network or the Centre for Creative Leadership, I am obliged to contract with the minimum terms of the international code to which they subscribe, which is that of the International Coach Federation. However, I am a South African first, and then a citizen of the world. I would therefore like to share how the ethics of the South African Comensa have guided me thus far in my coaching practice. Please feel free to visit the websites of these two organisations to read more about their approach to ethics:

- www.comensa.org.za
- www.coachfederation.org

Core coaching values

In particular, **inclusivity, dignity** and **integrity** are three of the coaching values that I strive to uphold. Firstly, I present the meanings as they are described in the Comensa code of ethics and then I explain how they guide my coaching conduct.

Inclusivity

Coaches will conduct themselves in a way that demonstrates an understanding of and respect for the dignity and diversity of all people – and also shows commitment to the transformation of South Africa and the promotion of equal opportunities for all.

Dignity

It is the primary responsibility of the coach to provide the best possible service to the client and to act in such a way as to cause no harm to any client or sponsor.

For me, these two values translate into a duty to regard any new client in a positive way from the time we meet. Moreover, I attempt to put aside my own preconceived ideas as far as possible. I generally achieve this mental state through mindfulness exercises. This skill needs my ongoing vigilance to achieve the best possible outcomes with my client.

Through reflection at the beginning and end of each session, I determine the mental state of my client at that point. My aim is to always leave clients in a better state than the one in which I found them, even if only small positive improvements have been made. As the process moves on, the biggest joy I experience is seeing clients lift their own ceiling of possibility and reach new levels of insight, personal growth and transformation.

Integrity

This value requires the coach to remain committed to functioning from a position of integrity, professionalism and personal responsibility. As one of the fundamental principles of ethics, integrity holds all coaches accountable for their conduct.

The pursuit of continuous improvement not only relates to supply chain or production practices. I have come to accept that it takes a keen sense of awareness and willingness (on my part) to get client feedback and to maintain discipline, and to constantly raise my own bar with regard to ethical thinking and acting. My clients open their minds and hearts to me with what they consider precious information. And so I continue to feel humbled to be allowed to work with them in deep and meaningful ways. The interaction is a privilege granted to me and something l will always value greatly. Should I ever err in the course of my work, I will learn from the experience and move forward with an improved set of coaching skills.

WHOSE ETHICS ARE RELEVANT?

One of my peers asked a profound question during a supervision session: "Whose ethics or values should be used as the measurement when working with company values?" After much debate, we concluded that there was not one single answer and that it required those leading the organisation to decide on the values they felt comfortable with and could endorse freely.

My role as team coach, on various projects mentioned in this book, was to ensure that the leaders I worked with used coaching as the vehicle to reach agreement on the selection of the values and ethical standards to be included in the plans they drew up. Contracting with my clients included my commitment to ethical coaching conduct on top of a healthy measure of personal values and beliefs (co-agreed by client and coach).

ETHICAL CHALLENGES DURING TEAM COACHING PROJECTS

In one of the cases documented in this book, the client organisation had recently undergone major restructuring, but was still in transformation. Interestingly, this was the first time that the client had assigned an investigation to an outside coach. In essence, the executive team wanted to determine how stakeholders felt about the organisation and management, with a focus on internal customers, mainly employees. The issue was a sensitive one, with the potential to create differences of opinion and conflict. In other words, it was likely to produce ethical dilemmas. The executive team reported a united willingness to explore how people perceived their organisational culture, and had no objections to my writing up the process and results of this project.

A dilemma may be described as a situation in which a choice has to be made between two or more unfavourable or unattractive alternatives, with ethical implications inherent in each choice. This situation crops up regularly during the course of my work. My approach to rendering meaningful results to the client organisation includes entering into a formal agreement with the executive team concerned.

At the same time I have the responsibility, as coach, of dealing with sensitive issues in a confidential and professional manner. Formal agreements or contracts are used to address ethical issues and to specify measurable outcomes with deadlines, as well as the roles to be played by both coach and client.

When a practising coach does research in any organisation, the publication of findings and results must be contractually agreed by all the key stakeholders. However, the real names of the individuals involved in the studies should not be published without permission. Also, it goes without saying, the content (and records) of coaching sessions are to be kept confidential at all times. A general principle to follow with regard to confidentiality is to always have a formal written agreement signed by all parties involved in the coaching intervention.

Often, my position in the client company is that of an independent consultant and outside coach. I do not wish to become an employee, and therefore have no vested interest in the results of the project; I have to determine the process that could ensure alignment in the team. Defining roles, responsibilities and boundaries is an important part of one's contract with clients.

When working with a team, the coaching role is not the only one you play. The coach often needs to share knowledge or facilitate a session, which enables the team to obtain clarity, reach consensus or clear the air. For this reason I have found it best to contract all the various roles that I may play during the process and the ones my clients need to play in order to ensure successful implementation. It is crucial that everyone involved knows how these roles are similar or different and when they need to be played, and it must be made explicit when roles change. For example, these are some of the roles I agree to when working with teams around alignment:

- Facilitator: I facilitate group processes aimed at discovering, discussing, understanding and deciding the indicators of the company culture.
- Trainer: I use a trustworthy and valid questionnaire to determine both the existing and the preferred cultures within this team. It calls for knowledge and skill to complete, score and interpret the results.

- Coach: I support individuals as well as the group to reflect on the meaning of values and behaviours (beliefs, sentiments, emotions and actions).

With regard to ethical conduct in a coaching context, contracting with the client in terms of ethics and confidentiality is without doubt the very first step in building a trusting and open relationship. In my personal coaching model (shared with you in chapter 3), contracting happens during either the first or second session, and after a shared understanding has been reached regarding the issues to be addressed.

To remain true to my own ethical code for coaching, scripts and recordings made of individual coaching sessions during this project are not given in this book. Only my personal summaries and my own reflections on the sessions are included as part of the content.

Some of the key elements that constitute my personal contract as coach to my client are the company mission statement, the company philosophy and its current business practices and company beliefs. When working with teams, it is useful to agree on a code of conduct that deals with matters of confidentiality and privacy, and to include this in the contract.

The content of the above elements constitutes a statement of intent that represents my signature presence, pointing to what I bring to the coaching relationship.[70] It offers the client a unique approach based on the personal values that underpin ethics and confidentiality for me. I leave room for the client to add their own value statements to the agreement.

There is a mutual understanding that if any of the client's values and life orientation are in conflict with my own personal beliefs and orientation, I will reconsider the appropriateness of my coaching services and refer the client to another coach.

With regard to confidentiality, I specifically record in my contracts that the coach may have to access in-depth knowledge and information relating to the operations of the client and the company. I further acknowledge that if such information is made available to any competitor (or used by me personally), the company would likely incur damage or loss and have its competitive edge compromised. Accordingly, my coaching contract stipulates that all documentation and material used for coaching must be treated with confidentiality. Moreover, these documents must be returned to the client upon completion of my coaching services.

In addition, I agree to maintain the utmost confidentiality while fulfilling my role as coach.

Both my position within the client organisation and the roles I am expected to play highlight the need for self-reflection, which is defined by Wolf in Merriam[71] as having the sensitivity, self-awareness and confidence to understand how the research process is unfolding and distinguishing between decision and recognition, with a focus on the latter. I make a conscious effort to reflect upon every single event that requires my interaction with either an individual client or with the full executive team of the organisation.

While managing coaching projects, I am alert to human subjectivity (my own and that of my client) and the power of perception (as the only reality). I am aware of the tension created in me when playing the various roles I have described, and I am mindful that I need to take care not to confuse the roles and thus perhaps render unreliable results. I see it as imperative that I constantly remind myself and my client of roles in every setting so that I can manage my clients' expectations and also maintain my own objectivity.

As an example of my ethical behaviour at Viking Enterprises, I made sure of my readiness to use my coaching approach in an ethical way by undertaking to comply with the following principles:

- Aim to be authentic with my client in the application of my own coaching approach.
- Contract individually with each member of the executive team in terms of the confidentiality of our relationship, over and above having contracted the confidentiality of the overall findings in the agreement mentioned earlier.
- Know what informs me, and share that information openly with my client.
- Have clarity on the purpose of coaching, my own beliefs, values and perceptions.
- Practise my own unique approach to coaching, which can potentially confirm that the client's acceptance will be forthcoming.

I believe that most executive teams are more than capable of communicating a vision of their preferred culture and values that matches their wishes for the future. But to ensure success, I have to be true to my principles as listed above. As coach, I have to remain proficient at facilitation in order to confirm the **existing** and the **preferred culture** and the cultural indicators with the executive team.

As a key ethical consideration, I always have to ensure that any process that is developed for a client organisation fits the purpose of the client. In the case of Viking Enterprises, the purpose was for the executive team to reach agreement on the preferred organisational culture.

For me, the bottom line is that my quest for continued growth and a heightened sense of awareness is ongoing – as is my undertaking to learn from any mistakes along the way. To withdraw from exploring, experiencing and venturing is to die slowly. But to try, fail, try again and succeed is to be fully alive and growing.

CONCLUSION

Cynthia Schoeman, the MD of Ethics Monitoring & Management Services (Pty) Ltd, explains that many organisations still engage in the exclusive pursuit of maximising shareholder wealth. "However, this is increasingly being judged against a more broadly ethical approach that views success in terms of outcomes for others as well"[72]. Cynthia's statement reminds me once again of my ongoing purpose: to be a mirror for clients who want to reconsider doing business in pursuit of sustainable results and want to take another look at their triple bottom line.

A very useful document on principles and the achievement of a multi-stakeholder focus to ponder with clients is one produced by the Corporation 20/20 initiative of the Tellus Foundation in the United States of America. Among other things, they include accrual of fair returns to customer, the equitable distribution of wealth among those who contribute to its creation, and sustainable operations for the benefit of both current and future generations (World Economic Forum Global Agenda Council on Values[73]).

Chapter 11

A SNAPSHOT OF MY MOST PROFOUND PERSONAL LEARNING AND REFLECTIONS TO DATE

INTRODUCTION

This chapter focuses on some of what I learnt as a coach, especially while working with alignment in teams. I highlight the cultural aspects that informed my coaching and critically review the usefulness (or value) of what I learnt for me, and for other organisations intent on implementing similar coaching initiatives. The chapter also speaks to those of you who are doing research in coaching.

Finally, I share some learning points and personal reflections that will hopefully provide the impetus for future research in the area of alignment.

LEARNING AND REFLECTION

According to Paulo Freire[74], author of the book *Education for Critical Consciousness*, learning can be both an active and a reflective process. Freire states that we tend to learn in many ways, not only through activities such as doing, constructing and writing, but also by thinking about experiences, which then adds to the learning. This confluence of experience and reflection combines to create new knowledge. We can therefore conclude that both action and reflection are essential ingredients in the construction of knowledge. The two elements are inextricably bound because we often reflect on activities as we perform them.

My personal reflective practice starts with preparing for a session and is ongoing during a session, whether it be mentally noted, physically felt and/or written down. At the end of each coaching session, I usually ask my clients to verbalise or write down what they think they have learnt from the session and its activities, and to share it with me, either in the moment or electronically later. In that way, a session is concluded with both parties being on the same page regarding the meaningfulness of the session. It also helps me to assess to what extent learning has taken place and to decide if the goals of the session were reached.

Double-loop reflection (reflections upon reflections) is an extremely useful technique to use a few days after coaching. The essence of this is that clients begin to understand their thinking and how thinking translates into actions and, ultimately, into results or consequences. The human brain takes time to integrate new learning, and it is when we are quietly reflecting on the events of the day or the day before that we become aware of patterns, habits and tendencies that we can then elect to repeat or discard.

The reflections expressed in this chapter are my personal reflections as coach, facilitator and trainer. As I have said before, I play various roles with various clients. Sometimes, I play various roles in one organisation, depending on the client needs and the brief I have been given.

I would like to mention again that I have discovered it is essential at the start of every intervention with a group to be explicit about the specific role that I will be playing during the course of that intervention. For instance, when there is a need to transfer knowledge, I remind participants that this role is different from that of the facilitator or the coach in the sense that transferring knowledge involves a combination of lecturing and teamwork. At other times, when I am asked for advice, I find it useful to remind them that my role can be more directional in nature than that of a team coach, which is more facilitative (to my mind).

This clarification is important for various reasons. Firstly, it is educational. Everyone is clear on the meanings of the various roles. Secondly, the expectations of the participants are more realistic, and thirdly, the role clarification acts as a self-check to make sure that I keep my coaching role as "pure" as possible.

I realise that I have developed this practice to ensure that the client knows what to expect of me and vice versa. For instance, should a team gather to take a crucial decision or resolve differences, I believe that my role should be that of facilitator. In my book, a facilitator brings "process" while the participants in the group or team bring "content". For them to take ownership for their decisions or solutions, they need to have generated them themselves. As team coach my brief may be more varied, but with a focus on achieving a state of shared and agreed meaning.

Reflection is a form of mental processing

Roger Schank[75] points out the importance of stories in learning and says that recalling and creating stories are part of learning. In fact, stories engage all parts of the brain. Zull (based on Moon[76]) points out that learning is deepest when it engages most parts of the brain. Moon, one of the most recent researchers on reflective practice at the time, provides the following definition:

Reflection is a form of mental processing – like a form of thinking – which we use to fulfil a purpose or to achieve some anticipated outcome. It is applied to relatively complicated or unstructured ideas for which there is not an obvious solution and it is largely based on the further processing of knowledge and understanding and possibly emotions that we already possess[77].

Storytelling as a form of reflection

As coaches, we can co-create stories with our clients. Teams can also create wonderful stories together as a way to construe collective meaning from their past or current situation, context and culture.

Donald Schön[78] says "storytelling is the mode of description best suited to transformation in new situations of action … stories are products of reflection, but we do not usually hold onto them long enough to make them objects of reflection in their own right". The author goes on to say that when we do get into the habit of recording our stories, we should revisit them later and attend to the meanings we built into them and to our techniques of narrative description.

For those of you who may consider the term **"storytelling"** too informal, note that Mattingly[79] recommends using the term **"narrative enquiry"**. He points to Aristotle's use of narrative as the natural framework for representing the world of action. Mattingly also elaborates on the "everyday sense-making role of storytelling"[80]; that stories reveal the way ideas look in action. Narrative provides explanation, he says. Our motivation for telling stories is really to wrest meaning from our experiences.

Clandinin and Connelly[81] call stories "unpretentious narrative". Stories are a fundamental method of personal growth through reflection, which is preparation for the future and deliberation on past considerations. Reflection does not always have to be in written form. For some students, reflections can be oral, shared with peers or teachers. However, as Schön[82] notes, we need to capture those stories in our portfolios to make them objects of reflection. With the addition of multimedia technologies, the stories can be captured in either audio or video format.

Janice McDrury and Maxine Alterio[83], two educators from New Zealand, have written a book called *Learning through Storytelling* in which they outline their theory of storytelling as an effective learning tool. They have linked the art of storytelling with reflective learning processes that are supported by literature on reflection and learning. They also see storytelling as a means of giving meaning to experiences.

My clients are often from an engineering background. As such, they are good at being action-oriented and are indeed goal-directed, but they have little inclination to pause, reflect and document their innermost feelings (of all things). Such learning and reflections become particularly influential in sustaining my journey of discovery. I find that I am fast developing greater skills as a professional coach. It's a good feeling!

KEY LEARNING ABOUT THE USE OF COACHING TO DISCERN ORGANISATIONAL CULTURE

My learning over the past decade is reflected in the discussion below.

Coaching is an excellent vehicle for investigating perceptions, views, fears and expectations about deep-seated issues of personal values and how to live these out in the workplace. I personally believe coaching is the best way to get a team of diverse people to agree on the leadership practices that should be displayed to entrench a new and preferred organisational culture within a relatively short period of time, provided that a safe space is created, confidentiality is agreed on and care is taken to keep everyone open-minded and included.

Teams I have worked with often demonstrated the value of healthy peer pressure. Even though some cultures do not reinforce intense competition, the principle of personal responsibility is inculcated from a young age in European cultures, resulting in a high level of maturity to do what needs doing without being prompted. This attribute of personal responsibility is extremely helpful for teams wanting to align themselves, as it fosters a sense of co-ownership and responsibility for any plan of action regarding the preferred organisational culture.

The combined coaching approach that I have followed since the turn of the century to reach consensus through meaningful conversation has been instrumental in coming to an agreement. The main reason for this success is that my approach fosters an environment within which team members can openly express their perceptions, knowing they are being heard and confident that their opinions are taken into account.

The above realisations have led to a substantial development in my approach, and I have subsequently rolled out the process distilled in this book many times over. I have applied my process in a variety of companies of different sizes, and within varying contexts. Work teams in my country are culturally diverse in dimensions such as language, race, gender, sexual orientation and even in levels of education and ingrained self-motivation.

Looking back on my experience with Viking Enterprises in particular, I am grateful for the opportunity to have worked with a homogenous cultural team. The added complexity of working with diverse cultural teams has, in recent years, certainly challenged and honed my personal growth as team coach.

THE USE OF QUESTIONNAIRES TO DETERMINE CURRENT AND PREFERRED ORGANISATIONAL CULTURE

I feel that the use of a valid and reliable cultural questionnaire can significantly jump-start a process of alignment towards a preferred culture and new leadership practices. There is a proviso, though. The questionnaire must focus on what is important for the organisation in question. This is especially the case with teams that represent a variety of organisational cultures, even when found within the same organisation. When the many different cultures have their own cultural jargon, there is usually a common language for constructs that may have different names in different parts of the organisation.

The wisdom of Harrison[84] and Harrison and Stokes[85] has proved very appropriate when linking an organisation's culture to its mission in order to facilitate buy-in and participation from all the relevant parties. The Viking Enterprises team saw such a close link between strategy and culture that they voluntarily added cultural dimensions to the strategic goals on one of the BSCs.

TEAM COACHING

At this stage, I use the term "team coaching" tentatively, because I still have to distinguish clearly between group facilitation and team coaching. The processes are similar in that both aim to provide space for a group of people to progress from a current state to a preferred state, with an end goal that has been agreed by all. The definition I provide below fits both coaching and facilitation.

As a result of having to wear different hats in different situations in my coaching practice, I distinguish between team coaching and facilitation. I consider it useful to reflect on my own distinction between these two competencies, as well the timing of each application during the course of most coaching projects. Firstly, I differentiate between the two and then determine the basis for my distinction by reviewing my reflective notes. On close scrutiny, the two concepts seemed to distinguish themselves (in my mind) in terms of their purposes and outcomes.

In figure 11.1, I illustrate why I found the two concepts to be appropriate in different settings during the course of the Viking Enterprises project.

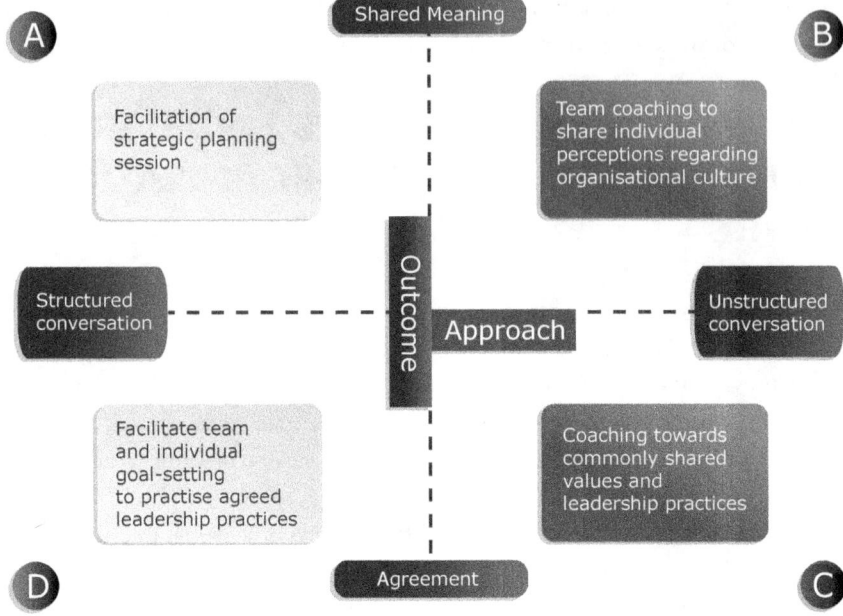

Figure 11.1: Illustrating the differences between facilitation and team coaching

Quadrant A describes the structured approach I use to facilitate the process whereby the executive team decides their future vision, mission and BSC. Quadrant B describes the team coaching approach used to allow a safe space for the sharing of meaning. It also allows for shared meaning to emerge and to be understood.

The alignment process evolves further in Quadrant C through team coaching (unstructured conversations among team members) to the point where the team reaches consensus on how and why the future organisational culture would be more meaningful. In Quadrant D, a more structured facilitative approach is used to allow team members to set the necessary team and individual goals to be achieved through agreed leadership practices.

A key lesson for me has been that team coaching followed by individual coaching works very well to achieve alignment. After agreeing on the priority issues needing attention, the executive team divides into smaller work teams. The effect on the levels of cooperation is always a positive one. Also, it gives impetus to move the process forward. The outcome is empowering to the team in that it results in individuals taking ownership and responsibility and also provides the opportunity to facilitate follow-up sessions.

An interesting observation about a code of conduct, which should be agreed at the outset, is that it should be defined before key issues are addressed. The code cuts across critical issues such as communication, commitment and responsibility, as well as information management, and thus helps to shift traditional boundaries that create ongoing dissatisfaction.

Teams make significant progress towards the agreed preferred culture in terms of leadership behaviour displayed during meetings when they develop and reinforce a code of conduct. Everyone seems more supportive when they take part in deciding on preferred conduct during team sessions, and are thus focused on achieving results.

INDIVIDUAL COACHING

When we coach executives in teams, we deal with each executive's perception of his or her own resourcefulness and willingness to commit to agreed leadership practices. Some reflection on the matter confirms my original thinking that the agreement of a preferred organisational culture is closely related to the commitment of leaders to reviewing their personal values. For me, this was a key lesson.

When I started out with my team coaching followed by individual coaching, I made the mistake of coaching both the team and the individuals. The execution of the team coaching and the personal coaching of all team members was more demanding than I had imagined. To keep all discussions within the boundaries of the coaching forum was taxing, but very rewarding in the end. I walked away feeling a sense of dignity, having enhanced my credibility with the client organisation. Nowadays, I firmly separate these roles and do either team coaching or one-on-one coaching, since this ensures that boundaries, being those of confidentiality (on behalf of the client) and those of resourcefulness (on the part of the coach), are maintained.

HOW TO ENSURE ETHICAL CONDUCT THROUGHOUT COACHING PROCESSES

My personal coaching ethics help me to achieve meaningful results, but at the same time I deal with sensitive issues in a confidential and professional manner. My signed agreement with the executive team of the client organisation facilitates my delivery of ethical conduct because:

- Matters of confidentiality and ownership of findings are clarified in advance.
- The expected measurable outcomes are clearly specified with deadlines, as are the roles of the researcher and the client.

USING A PROJECT APPROACH

Following a project approach to manage the coaching process is of value in providing an initial broad outline to a client, with the purpose of agreeing a timeline for implementation. This is especially useful when dealing with an action-oriented client who insists on measuring results in terms of time, and who expects feedback on progress at regular intervals. Furthermore, a project approach ensures measurable results and proper follow-through from both sides.

THE USE OF RECORDINGS, TRANSCRIPTS AND REFLECTION

The voice recordings I make of almost all the coaching sessions help me to formulate reflections on my coaching approach and on the outcomes achieved through that coaching.

With one client, the intention was that every member of the executive team would keep a diary to record his or her perspectives on the coaching events and the feelings he or she had in relation to them. Members also had to generate insights into the coaching process itself. In reality, the executive members were either too busy to keep diaries, or did not think it appropriate to write down their reflections. I then substituted reflective questions for coaching diaries to encourage reflections "in the moment". I introduced this aspect at the end of the coaching session (group and one-on-one). I also started every coaching session with questions that prompted or forced reflection on the previous coaching session, just in case any reflections had changed or perhaps deepened since the last session.

AN OBJECTIVE LOOK AT THE FEASIBILITY OF THIS COACHING PROJECT

Looking back on any study, one always agonises over issues that may have facilitated or complicated the research. Here are a few factors that do facilitate the successful implementation of coaching projects.

Credibility with the client organisation

I found that having previously consulted to or coached in a client organisation or knowing some of the people in the client organisation can either help or hinder your progress. A lot depends on the outcomes of the previous involvement with that client. If your previous projects were delivered successfully, you could well have a head start. The essence here is that of relationship-building! It can do you good if your new relationship with a client is poised to continue from a solid foundation of mutual respect and trust.

Complicating factors

A few of the factors that complicated the Viking Enterprises project are discussed below.

Difference in values

Right from the outset of any coaching, I expect my client to challenge my principle of not giving specific advice. Challenge it they do! Some organisations are so used to the more direct approach of consultants that they find it hard to have a facilitator or coach who expects them to come up with all the answers. Coaching means that you are facilitating a process in which the client organisation should find its own direction and generate its own options and solutions.

Language differences

The most difficult coaching I have ever undertaken was that with the MD of Viking Enterprises, mainly because of the language barrier. He spoke and understood little English, and as a result my coaching sessions with him were short. Consequently, I did not achieve the same depth of understanding of his perceptions of the preferred culture as I achieved with members of his team. I vowed never to coach someone through the use of a translator again. However, I would be comfortable coaching people in their second language.

Timeframe

A key lesson for me has been to always make sure that the client organisation has a proper business strategy in place before I work with them on their organisational culture and leadership practices. Should they not have one, I prefer that they work with someone else to get this in place before I agree to serve as coach for the cultural alignment. I thus ensure role clarity, which is essential for the establishment of openness and mutual understanding.

Playing multiple roles

Playing multiple roles such as those of facilitator, trainer, consultant and coach usually poses no challenge for me, nor does switching roles when required. A complication arises when the client does not know quite what to expect from which role. That is why roles must be clarified vigorously and upfront to prevent unrealistic expectations from the parties involved. In fact, roles should be framed in the early contracting phase – in terms of the outcomes expected from my involvement with them, but more importantly perhaps, in terms of the roles each of us will play and the responsibilities we will take up in the coaching partnership.

Lessons for institutions considering coaching initiatives to change culture and values

Having a strategy in place is central to the success of an alignment of values and culture in any organisation. The rationale for this view stems purely from my personal experience, as explained in earlier chapters. Strategy determines what needs to be done and culture determines how things are done.

Consulting experience has taught me that a client's dissatisfaction often stems from the way he or she was treated. The client may be unhappy even though the project was delivered within the time and cost parameters. Any organisation that is results-driven should resonate with a project planning approach to coaching.

Allowing the coach to play the role of coach, and not expecting that coach to consult, should foster the desired perception that any coaching initiative is supportive rather than directive. The internal clients (company members) may feel more comfortable with a coaching initiative where the goals are personal and the results are kept private than one where desired outcomes are set up as the organisation's goals.

Where alignment is imperative, team consensus should precede individual coaching to ensure focus and energy direction on the part of the coach.

CONCLUSION

Thank you for sharing in my learning. Don't hesitate to share your own learning and reflections with your clients, peers and the coaching community at large. Coaching was born from a sense of abundance, I believe. We need to put on our brave shoes, experiment, embrace both successes and mishaps, and share what we discover as we truthfully, and with care, co-create meaningful contributions to our clients, their organisations and our industry.

APPENDICES

APPENDIX A: AGREEMENT WITH VIKING ENTERPRISES

	DATE:
Agreement between:	
Client:	
Coach:	
Direct stakeholders:	
Client organisation:	
Date of agreement:	
TABLE OF CONTENTS	**PAGE NUMBERS**
Title	
Aims	
Outcomes	
Scope	
Project feasibility	
Impact of project results on the client organisation	
Attachments: 1. ………………………….. (eg Gantt chart) 2. ………………………….. (eg Glossary of terms)	
DESCRIPTION OF PROJECT TO BE DELIVERED **Project title:** The use of coaching to obtain agreement regarding the preferred culture within the executive team of the client company **Project outcomes:** • better understanding of company culture and specifically the four main cultures described by Roger Harrison, and the feasibility of having a combination of cultures in one organisation • increased awareness of the perceptions of executives on other levels of the organisation regarding both the current and preferred cultures of the organisation	

- a preferred culture agreed upon by all the members of the executive team
- increased personal understanding of individual versus team perceptions of the preferred organisational culture
- a list of personal and team indicators that reflect the preferred culture within the company
- a set of personal (individual) and team goals aimed at implementing indicators that would facilitate positive growth towards the development of the team's preferred culture

Project scope:

The scope of work will be focused mainly on the executive team of the client company. Another team of staff members on lower levels of the organisation will be included in the cultural survey part of the project, for purposes of comparing the existing and preferred cultures in the organisation.

Roger Harrison's diagnostic cultural questionnaire will be used to identify the existing and preferred cultures within the organisation.

A coaching process will be developed, consisting of both group and individual coaching interventions, aimed at:

- ensuring buy-in and commitment to the complete research process
- facilitating understanding of the four cultures measured in the Roger Harrison cultural questionnaire
- establishing the meaning of "own" versus "team" perceptions of culture and values
- reaching agreement on the preferred culture in the organisation and
- exploring indicators that reflect the preferred culture

Roles to be played by the coach:

- Facilitator: The coach will facilitate group processes aimed at discovering, discussing, understanding and deciding on the cultural indicators of the company culture.
- Trainer: A questionnaire will be used to determine both the existing and preferred cultures within the executive team. Team members will need specific knowledge and skills to complete, score and interpret the results, and even more importantly, to understand the results.
- Coach: The coach will support the group and individuals within it, and help them reflect on the meaning of values and behaviours (beliefs, sentiments, emotions and actions).

Relationship of coach to client company:

- The position of the coach will be that of an independent outsider.
- The client company will hire the coach for one year only.
- The research conducted in this organisation will form part of the package for which the coach will be paid. The coach is thus not an insider researcher; this is the continuation of a relationship which started two years ago, and is based on mutual goodwill and recognition of what we have achieved together to date.

TOOLS AND TECHNIQUES USED TO COLLECT AND ANALYSE DATA

Questionnaire on organisational culture by Roger Harrison:

Two sample groups will complete a questionnaire to diagnose the organisation's culture – the executive team of the Epsilon client company and another, randomly chosen group of executives on lower levels of the client company.

The rationale behind this is that the executive core of the organisation should be able to compare its views with those of its internal customers (employees) so as to determine any significant gaps in perception. However, only the executive team will be included in the coaching intervention.

Coaching:

For the purposes of this research, a coaching process will be devised that will foster agreement among the members of the executive team on their preferred organisational culture.
To achieve this, a combination of group and individual coaching sessions will be held.

- Group coaching will be used as the means by which the values of the executive team, as reflected in the culture questionnaire, will be confirmed. The values of both the existing and preferred cultures apply.
- Group coaching will also verify the behaviours that underpin the values reflected by both the existing and preferred cultures.
- Individual coaching sessions will be held to increase understanding of the research process, ensure support for it and establish goodwill with every member of the executive team.
- Individual coaching sessions will be held for the purpose of establishing the meaning of the individual's personal values, and how these relate to the values of the group.

Diary:

A diary will be kept to log significant experiences and insights prior to, during and after each interaction. Furthermore, **participants who receive coaching will be asked to keep a diary describing their own experiences of the process.** I hope that the involvement of participants throughout the whole process will provide the necessary incentive for them to log significant and useful data. I also hope that participant's diaries will reveal the writer's angle on events and the feelings they have had in relation to them. It should also give insight into the coaching process.

ADDITIONAL BENEFITS TO THAT OF INFORMING THE CLIENT ORGANISATION

- aligned thinking with regard to the future business of the organisation
- practical guidelines to all employees regarding the behaviour necessary to reach the organisation's business goals
- more awareness of the brand that the company represents

PROJECT FEASIBILITY

The coach has the following necessary skills and knowledge to carry out this research in order to complete this project successfully:

Knowledge:

- how to properly apply Roger Harrison's cultural questionnaire to ensure the collection of reliable data
- how to analyse and interpret the data rendered by this questionnaire (data analysis)
- how to give feedback to stakeholders in a meaningful, practical and encouraging way
- how to conduct group and individual coaching sessions

Skills:

- influencing skills to ensure that as many people as possible complete the surveys
- coaching skills
- communication, negotiation, convincing and persuasive skills
- instilling trust in people who have no reason to trust or mistrust me
- gaining the goodwill of all stakeholders
- facilitation and training skills

RESOURCES REQUIRED TO SUCCESSFULLY IMPLEMENT THIS PROJECT

Human:

The informed consent of the sponsor of this project (Managing Director of the client company), in other words this signed document.
Openness and honesty, as well as the support of all the members of the executive team of the client organisation.

Time:

From .... to ....

This timescale is realistic (see process-flow diagram).
To complete the project, six complete working weeks are needed.

Typical schedule of a working week:

Group coaching on Monday morning (executive team and coach)
Individual coaching the rest of Monday, Tuesday and Friday (members of executive team one-on-one with coaches)

Tentative dates:

Location:

Client's premises (six different business units situated in ??) and coach's office.

Information:

The main source of information will be the people that form part of this project process. The biggest challenge for both coach and client will be to gain and maintain the trust, support and goodwill of all key stakeholders involved in this project (executive team members).

IMPACT OF PROJECT RESULTS ON THE CLIENT ORGANISATION

- a preferred culture, agreed by all members of the executive team of the organisation
- enhanced understanding of the meaning of culture and values, especially those indicators that are indicative of a specific culture
- agreed cultural indicators of both the existing and preferred cultures with the company
- agreed executive team performance plan, specifying the indicators necessary in order to facilitate growth towards the agreed preferred culture
- personal action plans, prepared by each individual member of the executive team, describing how they will achieve the agreed executive team performance plan
- enhanced awareness and understanding of the indicators/behaviour that reflect the presence/existence of a particular culture

CONFIDENTIALITY

Both parties agree that all information shared among the client, coach and members of the executive team will be treated with respect.

Decisions regarding the sharing of information discussed among coach, client and members of the executive team should carry the consent of all the relevant stakeholders.

PAYMENT TERMS AND SIGNATURES

APPENDIX B: COMPLETE BALANCED SCORECARD FOR THE VIKINGS

- Financial goals

- Learning and growth goals

- Customer goals

- Internal business process goals

Balanced Scorecard

Strategic Objectives

★ Financial

To ensure an uncomplicated business experience with the aim of providing a mutually beneficial business result/outcome for all involved, we need to:

* Achieve the financial independence of every business unit.

* Achieve an increased market share.

* Achieve a turnover of _____ .

* Achieve a profit margin of _____ .

* Achieve a financial capacity to handle orders of up to _____ .

* Monitor the performance of our business partners more closely.

* Reduce margin slippage on project to _____ .

* Increase our invoiced consulting hours to _____ .

Balanced Scorecard

Strategic Objectives

★ Learning and Growth

To offer technical services/total engineering solutions to manufacturing industries, we need to:

* Improve our project-handling experience.

* Improve our capacity to offer total solutions.

* Improve our ability to be flexible and uncomplicated.

* Refine project-reporting systems.

* Define and apply our competitive advantage.

Balanced Scorecard

Strategic Objectives

★ Customers

To be open to networking and partnering with our international counterparts, with a view to strengthening and developing long-term viable customer relationships by:

*   strengthening our reputation for quality and on-time delivery

*   retaining a strong supplier base

*   building even better relations with customers

*   strengthening our marketing presence and company image

*   strengthening our brand name

*   broadening our market base (different segments)

Balanced Scorecard

Strategic Objectives

★ Internal Business Processes

In order to continually develop our existing exceptional competence in both engineering and project delivery we have to:

* Develop a best-practice way of planning, monitoring and evaluating the project process.

* Develop cost-effective purchasing routines.

* Develop a strategic management process which includes every staff member within ....

* Continuously work smarter, faster and better.

APPENDIX C: CODE OF CONDUCT

1. Show respect by

    * being on time
    * listening
    * switching off mobile phones and laptops during meetings

2. Be honest and open.

3. See our time together as an investment.

4. Be present (body and mind).

5. Create agendas to incorporate everyone's ideas and send them out 48 hours prior to the meeting.

6. Take responsibility to air your views and challenge the views of others.

7. Meet for 50 minutes and break for 10 minutes, to allow for telephone calls to be made.

8. Keep to commitments in terms of

    * preparation for meetings
    * actions taken of commitments made during meetings

9. Keep a protocol (at least regarding decisions taken) and make sure everyone gets this the next day.

APPENDIX D: NEW PERFORMANCE MANAGEMENT FORM FOR VIKING ENTERPRISES

WORKING ENVIRONMENT	Do not agree	Agree partly	Agree mostly	Fully agree
COMPANY IMAGE				
I am aware of the vision, business strategy and goals of our company.				
Comments:				
Our image helps us to attract customers and good-quality employees.				
Comments:				
LEADERSHIP AND MANAGEMENT				
The leaders of this organisation focus on achieving a good business result.				
Comments:				
The management style is geared to building long-term partnerships with both customers and employees.				
Comments:				
DEPARTMENT/POSITION				
My work environment allows for growth and development.				
Comments:				
I get enough and the right type of information to do my work well.				

Appendix D: New performance management form for Viking Enterprises

Comments:			
I take part in the decisions which affect me personally.			
Comments:			
I get the necessary feedback from my manager and co-workers as to how I am doing.			
Comments:			

JOB-RELATED TASKS

I feel confident that I have enough competence to work in the areas/on the jobs where I am being placed.			
Comments:			
I experience a sense of achievement in my daily work.			
Comments:			
I have enough resources, ie facilities, software and hardware, to do my job.			
Comments:			
I feel that my contribution is valued by my peers and my manager.			
Comments:			
I get the support I need from my manager.			
Comments:			

LEARNING AND GROWTH – GOALS FOR THE NEXT 6–12 MONTHS			
Type of job/industry/customer: *Comments:*			
Project: *Comments:*			
Partnership: *Comments:*			
Other: *Comments:*			
ACHIEVEMENT NEEDS		**SUPPORT NEEDS**	
Explanation: In order for me to achieve my goals, I will need … an introduction to a client/a new software package/more authority to make decisions/more knowledge of …		Explanation: To support me in my attempts to achieve my goals, I will need … personal coaching from my immediate manager/to be situated closer to … /to get more regular feedback on how I am doing …	
Employee's needs:		Employee's needs:	
Manager's commitment:		Manager's commitment:	
COMPETENCE DEVELOPMENT PLAN – NEXT 6–12 MONTHS			
Competence needed	Type of learning activity	Resources necessary	Timing
Comments:			
Competence needed	Type of learning activity	Resources necessary	Timing
Comments:			

Appendix D: New performance management form for Viking Enterprises

Competence needed	Type of learning activity	Resources necessary	Timing

Comments:

Experience needed	Type of learning activity	Resources necessary	Timing

Comments:

WORK GOALS DURING THE NEXT 6–12 MONTHS:

FINANCIAL OR COST-RELATED GOALS:	MEASUREMENTS	A	PA	NA
Eg keep to the budget agreed with customer. Increase invoiced hours to __ per month.	SEK … timesheet			

CUSTOMER-RELATED GOALS:	MEASUREMENTS	A	PA	NA
Eg provide feedback on progress e-mails/reports/minutes. Provide complete budgetary quotation.	deadline/budget price agreed internally			

PROCESS-IMPROVEMENT GOALS:	MEASUREMENTS	A	PA	NA
Eg agree conditions at handover to shorten delivery time of ... by two weeks. Fix quality problems in	checklist Gantt chart evaluation form			

COMMENTS:

Date of this development discussion:

Immediate Manager:

Venue:

Time:

Both parties agree that the contents of this working document have been discussed, understood and agreed.

_____ _____
Employee   **Manager**

ENDNOTES

1. ICF, 2005:1.
2. Comensa, 2015.
3. Ungerer, Herholdt & Le Roux, 2012.
4. Heckroodt, 2013:160.
5. O'Flaherty & Everson, 2009:80–81.
6. O'Neill, 2000:17.
7. O'Neill, 2000:13.
8. Pavlina, 2007:1.
9. Hoffman, 2006:1.
10. Zwell, 2000:144.
11. Hudson,1999:180.
12. Charlton, 2007:178, 95.
13. Manning, 2001:49–50.
14. Gallagher, 2004:viii.
15. Bellingham, 2001.
16. Kahn, 2014:23.
17. Kahn, 2014:24.
18. Passmore, 2010:206.
19. Schein, 1985.
20. Taylor, 2005:xiv.
21. Hopkins, Hopkins & Mallette, 2005:2–3.
22. Gentile, 2010:xiv.
23. Pennington, 2006.
24. Bellingham, 2001:18.
25. Harrison, 1995:200.
26. Ungerer, Herholdt & Le Roux, 2013:269.
27. Hawkins, 2014:5.
28. Van Rhyn, 2005.
29. Collins, 2015.
30. Schein, 2004.
31. Mostert, 2012:58.
32. Deal & Kennedy, 1982.
33. Cameron & Quinn, 1999.
34. Kaplan & Norton, 2006.
35. Hopkins et al, 2005.
36. Cox, Bachkirova & Clutterbuck, 2011.
37. Ivancevich & Matteson, 1996:535.
38. Steed, 2013:23.
39. Lane, 1990.
40. O'Neill, 2000:231.
41. Broadwell, 1969.
42. Burch, 1970.
43. Conscious competence learning model, www.businessballs.com/consciouscompetencelearningmodel.htm
44. Lane, 1990:120.
45. O'Neil, 2000:17.
46. Collingwood, 2010.
47. Lewin, 1951.
48. Lewin, 1951.
49. Hovland, 2005.
50. De Bono, 1999.
51. Lane, 1990.
52. Scheepers, 2012:8.
53. Harrison, 1995: 346.
54. Whitmore, 2003:155.
55. Zohar & Marshall, 2004:28.
56. Harrison, 1995:8.
57. Harrison, 1987.
58. Rollins & Roberts, 1998:12.
59. Van Coller, 2007.
60. Adapted from Havengal & Edmonstone, 1999 and Rasiel & Friga, 2001.
61. **Havengal & Edmonstone, 1999.**
62. **Porter, 1985.**
63. **Rasiel & Friga, 2001.**
64. Adapted from Porter, 1985.
65. **Harrison & Stokes, 1992.**
66. **Harrison & Stokes, 1992.**
67. **Harrison & Stokes, 1992.**
68. **Harrison & Stokes, 1992.**
69. Kaplan & Norton, 2006.
70. O'Neill, 2000.
71. Wolf in Merriam, 2002:117.
72. Schoeman, 2014:27.
73. World Economic Forum Global Agenda Council on Values, 2013.
74. Freire, 1973.
75. Schank, 1991.
76. Moon, 1999.
77. Moon, 1999:page.
78. Schön, 1988:19–20.
79. Mattingly, 1991.
80. Mattingly, 1991:45, 998–1005.
81. Clandinin & Connelly, 1991:258–81.
82. Schön, 1988.
83. McDrury & Alterio, 2002.
84. Harrison, 1995.
85. Harrison & Stokes, 1992.

REFERENCES

Bellingham, R. 2001. *Corporate culture change*. Amherst, MA: HRD Press.

Broadwell, MM. 1969. *Teaching for learning*. The gospel guardian. [Online] Available: http://www.wordsfitlyspoken.org/gospel_guardian/v20/v20n41p1-3a.html Accessed: 3 May 2014.

Burch, N. 1970. The four stages for learning any new skill. [Online] Available: http://www.gordontraining.com/free-workplace-articles/learning-a-new-skill-is-easier-said-than-done/ Accessed: 10 May 2015.

Businessballs.com. *Conscious competence learning model*. [Online] Available: www.businessballs.com/consciouscompetencelearningmodel.htm Accessed: 12 August 2015.

Cameron, KS & Quinn, RE. 1999. *Diagnosing and changing organizational culture: Based on the competing values framework*. Reading, MA: Addison-Wesley Longman.

Charlton, G. 2007. *Bridging the gap: Creating synergy between employees and organisations of choice*. Randburg: Knowres Publishing.

Clandinin, DJ & Connelly, FM. 1991. Narrative and story in practice and research, in *The reflective turn: Case studies in and on educational practice*, edited by DA Schön. New York, NY: Teachers College Press: 258–81.

Coaches and Mentors of South Africa (Comensa). 2014. *What is coaching?* [Online] Available: www.comensa.org.za/ABOUT_US/What is Coaching.aspx Accessed: 3 July 2014.

Collins, M. 2015. *Partners for possibility: How business leaders and principals are igniting radical change in South African schools*. Randburg: Knowres Publishing.

Coaches and Mentors of South Africa (Comensa). 2015. *What is coaching?* [Online] Available: www.comensa.org.za/what-is-coaching Accessed: 3 July 2015.

Collingwood, C. 2010. *The new code of NLP: A paradigm shift in Neuro-Linguistic Programming*. [Online] Available: http://www.inspiritive.com.au/nlp/the-new-code-nlp/ Accessed: 4 May 2014.

Cox, E, Bachkirova, T & Clutterbuck, D. 2011. *The complete handbook of coaching*. London: Sage.

Deal, E & Kennedy, AA. 1982. *Corporate cultures: The rites and rituals of corporate life*. New York, NY: Addison-Wesley.

Deal, E. & Kennedy, AA. 1999. *The new corporate cultures*. New York, NY: Perseus.

De Bono, E. *Six thinking hats*. 1999. [Online] Available: www.debonogroup.com/six_thinking_hats.php Accessed: 16 June 2014.

Freire, P. 1973. *Education for critical consciousness*. New York, NY: Continuum.

Gallagher, RS. 2004. *The soul of an organisation: Understanding the values that drive successful corporate cultures*. Chicago, IL: Dearborn Trade.

Gentile, MC. 2010. *Giving voice to values: How to speak your mind when you know what's right*. London: Yale University Press.

Harrison, R. (ed.). 1987. *Organisation culture and quality of service: A strategy for releasing love in the workplace*. London: Association for Management Education and Development.

Harrison, R. 1995. *The collected papers of Roger Harrison*. London: McGraw-Hill.

Harrison, R & Stokes, H. 1992. *Diagnosing organisational culture*. San Francisco, CA: Jossey-Bass/ Pfeiffer.

Havengal, M & Edmonstone, J. 1999. *The facilitator's toolkit*. London: Gower.

Hawkins, P. 2014. High-performing teams – the latest research and development, in *Leadership team coaching in practice: Developing high-performing teams*, edited by P Hawkins. London: Kogan Page.

Heckroodt, S. 2013. *Strategic thinking game over: New rules for 21st century business*. Cape Town: Epubsa.co.za.

Hoffman, P. 2006. *Define your position: values, ethics & leadership*. [Online] Available: http://ezinearticles.com/?Define-Your-Position:-Values,-Ethics-and-Leadership&id=334934 Accessed: 15 July 2014.

Hopkins, WE, Hopkins, SA & Mallette, P. 2005. *Aligning organisational subcultures for competitive advantage: A strategic change approach*. New York, NY: Basic Books.

Hovland, I. 2005. *Successful communication: A toolkit for researchers and civil society organizations*. London: Overseas Development Institute. [Online] Available: www.change-management-coach.com Accessed: 10 May 2015.

Hudson, FM. 1999. *The handbook of coaching: A comprehensive resource guide for managers, executives, consultants, and human resource professionals*. San Francisco, CA: Jossey-Bass.

International Coaching Federation (ICF). 2014. *What is professional coaching?* [Online] Available: www.coachfederation.org/need/landing.cfm?ItemNumber=978&navItemNumber=567 Accessed: 3 July 2014.

International Coach Federation (ICF). 2005. [Online] Available: http://www.icfphiladelphia.org/what-is-coaching- Accessed 29 July 2015.

Ivancevich, JM & Matteson, MT. 1996. *Organizational Behaviour and Management*. Chicago, IL: Irwin.

Kaplan, RS & Norton, DP. 2006. *Alignment: Using the balanced scorecard to create corporate synergies*. Boston, MA: Harvard Business School.

Kahn, MS. 2014. *Coaching on the axis: Working with complexity in business and executive coaching*. London: Karnac Books.

Lane, DA. 1990. *The impossible child*. London: Trentham.

Lewin, K. 1951. *Field theory in social science: Selected theoretical* papers. New York, NY: Harper.

Manning, T. 2001. *Making sense of strategy*. Cape Town: Zebra Press.

Mattingly, C. 1991. The narrative nature of clinical reasoning. *American Journal of Occupational Therapy*, 45, 998–1005. [ebook] doi:10.5014/ajot.45.11.998. Accessed: 14 July 2014.

McDrury, M & Alterio, M. 2002. *Learning through storytelling: Using reflection and experience in higher education contexts*. New Zealand: Dunmore Press.

Merriam, SB. (ed.) 2002. *Qualitative research in practice: examples for discussion and practice*. San Francisco, CA: Jossey-Bass.

Moon, J. 1999. *Reflection in learning and professional development*. London: Kogan Page.

Mostert, M. 2012. *Systemic leadership learning: Leadership development in the era of complexity*. Randburg: Knowres Publishing.

O'Flaherty, C & Everson, J. 2009. Coaching in South Africa, in *Diversity in coaching: Working with gender, culture, race and age*, edited by J Passmore. London: Kogan Page: 80–81.

O'Neill, MB. 2000. *Executive coaching with backbone and heart: A systems approach to engaging leaders with their challenges*. San Francisco, CA: Jossey-Bass.

Passmore, J. 2010. *Excellence in coaching: The industry guide*. London: Kogan Page.

Pavlina, S. 2007. *Living your values*. [Online] Available: http://www.stevepavlina.com/articles/living-your-values-1-htm Accessed: 3 July 2014.

Pennington, R. 2006. *Results rule! Build a culture that blows the competition away*. Hoboken, NJ: John Wiley.

Porter, ME. 1985. *Competitive advantage: Creating and sustaining superior performance*. New York, NY: The Free Press.

Rasiel, EM & Friga, PN. 2001. *The McKinsey mind: Understanding and implementing the problem-solving tools and management techniques of the world's top strategic consulting firm*. New York, NY: McGraw-Hill.

Rollins, T & Roberts, D. 1998. *Work culture, organisational performance, and business success*. London: Quorum Books.

Schank, RC. 1991. *Tell me a story: A new look at real and artificial memory*. New York, NY: Atheneum.

Scheepers, C. 2012. *Coaching leaders: The 7 'P' tools to propel change*. Randburg: Knowres Publishing.

Schein, EH. 1985. *How culture forms, develops and changes*. San Francisco, CA: Jossey-Bass.

Schein, EH. 1997. *Organisational culture and leadership*. San Francisco, CA: Jossey-Bass.

Schein, EH. 2004. *Organisational culture and leadership*. San Francisco: Jossey-Bass.

Schoeman, C. 2014. *Ethics can: Managing workplace ethics*. Randburg: Knowres Publishing.

Schön, D. 1988. Coaching reflective teaching, in *Reflection in teacher education*, edited by P Grimmett & G Erickson. New York, NY: Teachers College Press: 19–20.

Schön, D. 1991. *The reflective turn: Case studies in and on educational practice*. New York, NY: Teachers College Press.

Steed, J. 2013. *Leadership: The catch-22 of high performance management*. [Online] Available: https://leadershape.wordpress.com/2013/01/22/leadership-the-catch-22-of-high-performance-management/ Accessed: 5 June 2014.

Taylor, C. 2005. *Walking the talk*. London: Random House.

Ungerer, M, Herholdt, J & Le Roux, J. 2012. *Leadership for all: Virtue practices to flourish*. Bryanston: KR Publications.

Ungerer, M, Herholdt, J & Le Roux, J. 2013. *Leadership for all*. Bryanston: KR Publications.

Van Coller-Peter, S. 2007. *The use of coaching to obtain agreement regarding the preferred culture within an executive team*. Unpublished DProf thesis. London: Middlesex University.

Van Rhyn, L. 2005. *Processes of culture change in organisations – the contribution of an external facilitator.* Unpublished PhD thesis. Hertfordshire: University of Hertfordshire.

Whitmore, J. 2003. *Coaching for performance.* London: Nicholas Brealey.

Wikipedia. 2014. *North Germanic languages.* [Online] Available:

http://en.wikipedia.org/wiki/North_Germanic_languages Accessed: 19 January 2015.

Wolff, RF. 2002. Self-reflection: an essential quality for phenomenological researchers, in *Qualitative research in practice: Examples for discussion and analysis*, edited by SB Merriam. San Francisco, CA: Jossey-Bass: 117.

World Economic Forum Global Agenda Council on Values. 2013. *A new social covenant.* [Online] Available: www.anewsocialcovenant.org Accessed: 19 January 2015.

Zohar, D & Marshall, I. 2004. *Spiritual capital: Wealth we can live by.* San Francisco, CA: Berrett-Koehler.

Zwell, M. 2000. *Creating a culture of competenc*e. New York, NY: John Wiley.

INDEX

A

accountability, 99
achievement and explanation of achievement, 102–104
achievement culture, 82, 83, 88
   strong, 98
actual coaching processes, 41, 51, 53
agenda, 102, 103, 107, 143
agreement, 11, 26, 35, 48–51, 53, 68, 69, 72, 73, 79, 83, 85–87, 99, 120, 133
   confidentiality, 81
   signed, 69, 129
   unanimous, 11, 62
aligning subcultures, 20
aligning teams, 2, 43
alignment, 13, 16, 17, 18, 19, 20, 23, 40, 41, 50, 53, 56, 118, 123, 132
   strategic, 90, 93
alignment process, 77, 128
   cultural, 70
Appendix, 50, 81, 91, 94, 95, 133, 138, 143, 144
application, 5, 6, 60, 71, 90, 120, 127
assessment centres, 29, 111
assessments, 7, 24, 29
attention, 29, 45, 73, 85, 86, 87, 89, 93, 128
authority, 88, 94, 106

B

balance, 7, 8, 34
Balanced Scorecard/s (BSC/s), 20, 70, 81, 91, 93, 97, 98, 102, 127, 128,139, 140–142
beliefs, 6, 8, 11, 14, 15, 16, 19, 20, 21, 23, 25, 62, 117, 119, 120
   personal, 49, 115, 119
Balanced scorecard for Viking Enterprises, 91, 138
belief systems, 14, 15
best coaching outcomes, 38
boundaries, 34, 63, 83, 85, 118, 129
   cultural, 29
   moral, 10
business, 4, 6, 18, 48, 49, 56, 59, 61, 69–70, 87, 89, 91–92, 100, 103, 112

cultures, 45
decisions, 11, 15
environment, 58
focus, 11, 49
goals, 54
leaders, 15, 19
organisation's business goals, 135
organisation-wide, 69
processes, 98, 99
project-orientated, 47
strategy, 20, 57, 131, 144
unit boundaries, 92
unit leader, 87
unit manager, 93, 96
unit strategies, 81, 96
units, 19, 20, 45, 48, 49, 53, 68, 69, 76, 80, 84, 85, 87, 88, 98
buy-in, 65, 127, 134

C

call organisational culture, 17
capacity, 9, 14, 15, 65, 103, 107, 140
case study, 66, 105, 109
challenges, 6, 25, 29, 32, 37, 40, 45, 61, 63, 69, 73, 74, 100, 104, 113
   ethical, 115, 117
change, 5, 7, 9, 11, 14, 17, 24–25, 34, 45, 48, 65, 67, 84, 99, 109
   cultural, 24
   culture, 132
   management interventions, 66, 67
   organisational, 19
   process, 66
choices, 5, 7, 13, 14, 24, 31, 40, 118
   personal, 13, 14, 37
citizens, second-class, 106
civil society organisations, 35
client company, 118, 133, 134, 135, 136
   feedback, 117
   groups, 20
   interaction, 31
   organisation, 72, 105, 106, 107, 117, 118, 119, 120, 129, 130, 131, 133, 135, 136, 137
   perceptions, 9

Index

realises, 40
relationship, 23
clients, 4, 5, 6, 7–10, 25–27, 31, 32–34, 36–38,
    116, 117, 118, 119, 120, 124, 129–133
  action-oriented, 130
  competent, 36
  executive-level, 40
  individual, 120
  internal, 132
  new, 116
  potential, 31
  progress, 33
  satisfaction, 9
  self-coaching, 38
  self-discovery, 4
  service, 3, 30
coach, 4–10, 24, 25–27, 31, 63, 113, 116, 117,
    118, 119, 124, 131, 132, 134, 136–137
  executives, 129
Coaches and Mentors of South Africa
    (Comensa), 4, 115–116
coaching, 3, 4–10, 23, 26, 27, 30–32, 37–38,
    49–51, 107, 111, 112, 113, 115–117, 126,
    131
  agreement, 43
  capacity, 29
  career, 10
  community, 63, 132
  conduct, 116
  contract, 119
  conversations, 32, 71, 79, 82
  diaries, 130
  endeavour, 54
  engagement, 26
  environment, 37
  ethical, 117
  events, 130
  executive, 44
  forum, 129
  individual, 44, 76, 86, 129, 132, 136
  initiatives, 123, 132
  journey, 4, 7, 25, 37
  key individuals, 45
  matrix, 73
  on-the-job, 111
  partnership, 131
  phase, 38
  practices, 23, 30, 116, 127
  projects, 43, 70, 104, 127, 130
  proposal, 50
  psychologist, 66
  required, 105
  role, 29, 118, 124
  services, 119
  sessions, 5, 7, 10, 33, 37, 54, 59, 61, 68,
      75–76, 79, 80, 118, 130, 131
  skills, 7, 117, 136
  small-team, 86
  steps, 50, 81
  style, 8, 33, 54
  values, 116
coaching cycle, 76
  complete, 76
  second, 74–75
coaching frameworks, 3, 23, 59
  personal, 7, 13, 41
coaching intervention, 30, 49, 68, 101, 106,
    109, 118, 135
  individual, 134
coaching model, 24, 29, 31, 33, 38
  author's, 38
  personal, 30–31, 119
coaching profession, 115
  expanding, 115
coaching relationship, 6, 8, 26, 27, 31, 68, 81,
    119
  constructive, 8
  professional, 27

coach leaders, 65
coach's efforts, 5
coach's responsibility, 4
coach's summary, 81
Cognitive Behavioural Coaching (CBC), 32
cohesive work teams, 29
combination, 3, 17, 44, 63, 71, 83, 93, 95, 98,
    124, 133, 135
  culture, 55
combined coaching process, 79
commitments, 8, 9, 75, 76, 80, 81, 97, 98, 106,
    107, 116, 117, 128, 129, 143
  following, 97, 98
company, 2, 3, 6, 7, 11, 16, 17, 20, 46, 47–50,
    59, 70, 101, 102, 119
  beliefs, 119
  culture, 47, 48, 50, 118, 133, 134

image, 141, 144
members, 132
performance, 112
status, 47
company strategy, 81
  comprehensive, 102
  new, 91
company values, 48, 70, 117
  new, 48–49
competence, 16, 28, 85, 95, 97, 99, 104, 113, 145, 146–147
  conscious, 28, 100
competitiveness, 17, 40
concepts, 6, 15, 24, 40, 45, 46, 127
  abstract, 14
conduct, 24, 46, 74, 75, 94, 116, 117
  code of, 74, 76, 81, 89, 94, 119, 128, 129, 143
  ethical, 62, 115, 119, 129
  new code of, 81
conduct group and individual coaching sessions, 54, 136
confidentiality, 31, 59, 69, 81, 115, 118, 119, 120, 126, 129, 137
conflict, 2, 10, 24, 26, 30, 35, 85, 99, 117, 119
conscious competence stage, 28
conscious competence theory, 27–28, 99–100
consensus, 70, 88, 118, 126, 128
consultants, 27, 32, 40, 88, 89, 95, 115, 131
content, 79, 88, 111, 118, 119, 124, 133, 148
contexts, 14, 31, 34, 41, 43, 51, 65, 104, 105, 125, 126
contract, 26, 32, 38, 106, 116, 118, 119, 120
contracting, 8, 10, 26, 38, 39, 53, 117, 119
contributions, 9, 10, 29–30, 40, 46, 61, 80, 84, 87, 94, 112, 113, 132, 145
control, 2, 9, 72, 101, 102, 103, 104
  oriented organisational culture, 58, 63
  procedures, 2
conversations, 5, 9, 25, 30, 55, 61, 66, 68, 76, 99, 102, 126
  one-on-one, 30, 31
cooperation, 40, 44, 56, 66, 76, 92, 95, 97, 100, 128
  better, 84, 92, 98, 101, 103
core coaching values, 116
core management team, 88
corporate cultures
  strong, 20
  weak, 20
corporate values act, 15
corporate world, 29
costs, 103, 109, 111
counselling, 31
country, 9, 19, 48, 107, 115, 126
credibility, 63, 129, 130
cultural
  backgrounds, 2, 30
  differences, 44, 45
  factors, 13
  focus, 11, 49
  jargon, 127
  outcomes, 90
  renewal, 25
  teams, diverse, 127
  training day, 94
cultural alignment, 19, 80, 93, 131
  goals, 97
cultural indicators, 98, 120, 134
  agreed, 137
cultural questionnaire, 134–136
  diagnostic, 134
  organisational, 71
  reliable, 127
culture
  acts, 15
  change, 14
  change initiative, 66
  questionnaire, 135
  shift, complete, 4
culture survey, 72
  organisational, 71, 72, 100
cultures, 3, 11, 14–17, 19, 44–45, 48, 49, 54, 55–57, 63, 68, 70, 71, 83, 137
  achievement-oriented, 74
  aligning, 53, 56
  cohesive, 46
  combined, 72
  common, 15, 80
  consistent, 61
  corporate, 13, 16, 20
  desired, 84
  distinct, 53
  diverse, 3
  given, 63
  homogenous, 45
  organisation's, 16, 72, 127, 135

role-orientated, 102
role-oriented, 72, 101
strong, 17, 20, 21
support, 61, 82, 94
support-orientated, 102
current culture, 18, 55, 56, 71, 75, 80, 102–104
  dominant, 63
customer feedback, 97, 100
customer-related goals, 147
customer relationships, 60, 141
customers, 15, 16, 17, 18, 48, 49, 60, 61, 66, 69, 97, 100, 104, 141, 144
  external, 62, 65
customer service, 17, 62, 65

D

Danish organisation, 66
decisions, 14, 40, 56, 62, 65, 85, 87, 88–90, 94, 95, 102, 103, 124, 143, 145
deficiency, 28
departments, 19, 20, 111
diagnose organisational culture, 62
dialogues, 19, 30
dignity, 116, 129
dimensions, cultural, 127
direction, 3, 5, 21, 27, 58, 59, 63, 80, 131
  strategic, 69, 97
discern organisational culture, 126
disciplines, 24, 25, 115, 117
dissatisfaction, client's, 132
distinctive organisational culture, 20
divisions, 45, 100, 110, 111, 112
  change management, 2
dominant control-oriented culture, 57
dominant organisational culture, 40
double-loop learning process, 24

E

emotions, 31, 33, 119, 125, 134
employees, 14, 15, 16, 20, 21, 49, 50, 56, 57, 68, 69, 98, 117, 135, 146
empowerment, 49, 85, 88
energises, 10, 19
environment, 4, 40, 58, 61, 102, 103, 104, 109, 126
  client's, 40

market, 60
ethics, 3, 69, 81, 115–117, 119
  code, 115
European cultures, 126
evaluating client, 33
executive coach, 10
  professional, 1
executive members, 2, 57, 66, 100, 130
executives, 1, 44, 45, 55, 56, 68, 83, 133, 135
executive team, 11, 49–51, 53, 54, 56, 61, 62, 69, 70, 71, 72, 73, 79–86, 120, 133–137
  complete, 69
executive team members, 62, 66, 72, 79, 83, 87, 100, 101, 137
executive team of Viking Enterprises, 50, 53, 62, 65, 79, 85, 100
executive team one-on-one, 136
executive team performance plan, 137
executive team scores, 82
executive team's perceptions, 54
expected individual coaching outcomes, 86
experiences, 3, 4, 5, 17, 23, 24, 25, 29, 69, 70, 116, 117, 123, 125, 126
  project-handling, 140

F

facilitation, 7, 15, 77, 97, 109, 120, 127, 128, 136
  strategic planning session, 128
facilitator, 29, 30, 35, 44, 61, 118, 124, 131, 134
feasibility, 50, 86, 97, 130, 133
feedback, 7, 37, 54, 59, 66, 72, 88, 93, 96, 97, 100, 107, 109, 111, 130
field, 10, 33, 44, 96, 101, 109, 115
  analysis, 33, 34, 99
final coaching cycle, 75
findings, 9, 10, 49, 50, 54, 59, 65, 75, 85, 107, 118, 120, 129
forcefield analysis of Viking Enterprises, 99
formal agreements, 53, 118
foundation, 4, 5, 6, 25, 29, 31, 45
frameworks, 14, 21, 23, 33, 36, 43, 113
functional managers, 106, 108

G

Gantt chart, 69, 70, 133

global coach network, 116
goals, 20, 21, 49, 50, 76, 77, 80, 81, 90, 96, 97, 98, 106, 107, 146
   common, 40, 55, 85, 90, 92, 102
   cultural, 76, 78
   customer, 138
   individual, 77, 128
   organisation's, 132
   strategic, 76, 90, 97, 127
   set, 99, 107
group, 14, 15, 44, 46, 47, 61, 62, 63, 73, 75, 82, 94, 124, 134, 135
   coach, 61
   processes, 118, 134
   representative, 71, 72, 82
   second, 53, 54, 79
   session, 61, 81
group coaching, 61, 135, 136
   processes, 78, 79
   sessions, 61, 62, 81
growth, 38, 76, 83, 85, 96, 97, 103, 106, 120, 137, 140, 144, 146
   long-term, 2, 10, 15, 16, 21
   personal, 8, 29, 116, 125, 127
   positive, 50, 76, 77, 90, 134
guide, 2, 6, 14, 15, 24, 34, 35, 79, 88, 116

H

Hall of Fame organisations, 20
Harrison's organisational survey, 49
hats, 35, 127
heart, 10, 14, 16, 57, 79, 106, 117
higher levels, 57, 62, 85, 92, 112
homogenous work teams, 2

I

implementation, 1, 20, 37, 38, 50, 68, 89, 109, 110, 111, 112, 113, 115, 118, 130
inclusivity, 111, 116
incompetence, 28
indicators, 16, 50, 55, 62, 71, 73, 83, 118, 134, 137
   behavioural, 56, 71, 73, 82
individual coaching approach, 63
   feedback, 87
   progress, 91

sessions, 54, 61, 62, 73, 75, 81, 93, 119, 135, 136
individual leaders, 97
individual perceptions, 54, 73, 86, 128
individuals, 5, 7, 13, 17, 25, 30, 85, 90, 99, 106, 108, 118, 128, 129, 134
induction programme, 96
industrial psychologist, 2, 6, 7, 29, 32
industry, automotive, 11, 44
influence, cultural, 83
information, 5, 35, 54, 62, 85, 89–90, 94, 96, 97, 99, 108, 119, 120, 137, 144
informs, 21, 24, 32, 33, 34, 37, 120
instrumental, 14, 71, 73, 126
integration, internal, 15
intentions, client's, 5
interaction, 5, 16, 19, 27, 33, 34, 35, 43, 46, 47, 117, 120, 135
interactive coaching process, 10
internal business processes, 142
internal business process goals, 138
International Coach Federation (ICF), 4, 116
international coaching bodies, 116
international organisation, 2, 30
intervention, 24, 39, 59, 67, 68, 85, 108, 124
   strategic, 70
interview, 47, 68, 69

J

job motivation, 85
journaling, 59
journals, 59, 76
journey, 3, 5, 23, 29, 55, 65, 68

K

key leadership challenges, 73
key lesson, 128, 129, 131
key organisational values, 20
knowledge, 13, 31, 111, 118, 123, 125, 134, 136

L

language barriers, 44, 45, 131
leaders, 1–2, 6, 13–21, 63, 65, 66, 83, 85, 88, 94, 95, 99, 102, 103, 104
leadership, 6, 17, 18, 32, 72, 73, 75, 76, 89, 98, 144

alignment, 18
behaviours, 57, 83, 129
issues, 74, 75, 86, 93
roles, 98
teams, 17, 24, 67
values, 23
leadership practices, 53, 54, 61, 62, 63, 76, 77, 84, 86, 90, 91, 96, 97, 101, 102
agreed, 86, 87, 96, 128, 129
critical, 72, 84, 86
demonstrated preferred, 73
following, 88, 89
improved, 73, 82, 86
new, 86, 127
leadership styles, 18, 54, 57, 67
individual, 63
learners, 7, 28, 109, 112, 113
learners/coachees, 112
learning, 3, 4, 5, 6, 23, 24, 27, 30, 37, 38–39, 109, 123, 124, 125–126, 132
key, 95, 126
transfer of, 7, 109, 112, 113
activity, 146–147
journey, 69, 80
new, 7, 45, 67, 96, 109, 112–113, 124
learning processes, 6
reflective, 125
learnt, 3, 7, 25, 26, 27, 33, 36, 40, 46, 69, 87, 107, 108, 110
learnt skills, 111
lessons, 3, 9, 39, 132
life, 3, 4, 6, 7, 14, 23, 31, 43
line managers, 108, 112, 113

M

management, 7, 54, 61, 90, 93, 103, 117, 144
behaviours, 75, 76
meetings, 92, 106, 107, 108
practices, sustainable project, 109
process, strategic, 142
style, organisation's, 59
tool, common project, 69
managers, 1–2, 10, 13, 16, 20, 21, 43, 92, 94, 95, 105–108, 110, 111, 112, 145
manager's commitment, 146
managing coaching projects, 120
managing director, 44, 45, 136

meetings, 41, 43, 44, 45–46, 49, 69, 85, 89, 94, 100, 102, 103, 107, 111, 143
members, 48, 54, 62, 63, 74, 75, 81, 82, 83, 86, 100, 130, 135, 136, 137
individual, 76, 94, 137
mental processing, 124–125
mentor, 4, 5
mentoring, 14, 115
merger, 2
milestones, 65, 68, 69, 70, 71, 72, 73, 76, 77, 79, 86, 99, 107, 108, 110–112
set, 68, 72, 78, 84, 86
misaligned subcultures demands, 21
modalities, 33
model, 3, 6, 9, 21, 23, 24, 27, 31, 41, 43, 113
motivation, 21, 85, 91, 92, 98, 99, 111, 125

N

neuro-linguistic programming (NLP), 33
new culture, 11, 63, 65, 66, 67, 84, 94, 97
envisaged, 97
planned, 54
not-for-gain umbrella organisation, 115

O

objects of reflection, 125
one-on-one coaching sessions, 4, 24, 41, 67, 68, 73, 81, 86, 93, 96, 97, 107, 129
openness, 55, 81, 103, 131, 136
organisation, 13, 14, 15, 16, 19–21, 25, 48–50, 53–56, 62, 66, 70–74, 82, 84, 95–98, 134
bigger, 4
petroleum, 110
organisational behaviour, 14
organisational culture, 2, 6, 16, 18, 19, 51, 54, 57, 71, 72, 74, 82–84, 127, 128, 131
current, 72
new, 2, 17, 41, 67, 76
strong, 21
weak, 21
organisational development, 24
organisational goals, 10, 17, 40
long-term, 1
organisational interventions, failed, 20
organisational levels, lower, 82
organisation focus, 144

organisation's ability, 16, 56
organisation's leaders, 16
organisation's problems, 27
orientation
  preferred cultural, 95
  supportive cultural, 95
outsider coach, 27
ownership, 13, 32, 37, 124, 128, 129

P

participants, 5, 55, 124, 135
parties, 8, 24, 26, 35, 39, 41, 44, 118, 127, 131, 137, 148
passion, 3, 6, 10, 31, 40, 43
peers, 18, 85, 94, 99, 105, 106, 117, 125, 132, 145
perceptions, 9, 29, 40, 41, 48, 50, 53–54, 71, 72, 82–84, 120, 126, 133, 134, 135
  cultural, 63
  personal, 55, 82
performance, 3, 4, 6, 13, 19, 29, 37, 45, 95, 96, 101, 102, 109, 139
  organisational, 20
  shared organisational values sustain, 17
performance management, 1, 95
  better, 95, 104
performance management strategy, current, 90
performance measurement forms, 95
performance measurements, 93, 95
personal coach, 57
personal coaching approach, 31
personal experience, 5, 16, 21, 132
personal learning, 123
personal value base, 2
personal values, 23, 31, 54, 55, 117, 119, 126, 129, 135
  living, 13
personal value systems, 2, 6
PESTLE analysis technique, 58–59
phase, 30–33, 36–38, 71, 72, 76, 81
policies/procedures, 99
power, 2, 10, 40, 82, 83, 85, 94, 98, 99, 120
  bargaining, 61
power culture, 82
practising coach, 118
practitioners, 19, 102, 115
preferred culture, 50, 53–54, 62, 63, 70, 71, 72, 73, 76, 77, 81–82, 84–86, 96–99, 101, 133–135

agreed, 21, 92, 129, 137
element, 85
goals, 57
preferred organisational culture, 11, 15, 55, 56, 72, 73, 75, 76, 77, 78, 79, 80, 84, 85, 126
process, 6, 19, 44, 45, 55–59, 62, 66, 68, 70, 75, 80, 81, 99, 107, 118
  autonomous, 30
  clumsy, 2
  creative, 4
  evolutionary, 15
  flow diagram, 136
  flow diagram, 49, 68
  improvement goals, 148
  intensive, 44
  planned, 51
  reflection, 5, 55
  reflective, 123
  team-coaching, 27
  tedious, 47
  transformation, 25
professional association, 4
  coach, 3, 6, 10, 11, 23, 126
  coaches, 5
  coaching, 4, 6, 11, 24, 47, 115
progress, 37, 59, 61, 74, 75, 76, 77–78, 87–88, 91, 92, 96, 109, 110, 112, 130
  client's, 5
  team's, 89, 90
project approach, 67, 109, 130
project delivery, 60, 104, 142
project evaluation subgroups, 92
project feasibility, 133, 136
project leaders, 103
project leadership, 111
  competent, 112
project management, 49, 67, 93, 96, 103, 104, 110, 111, 113
  background, 113
  capacity, 110
  experiences, 3
  programmes, 110
  strategy, 103
  system, 93
project management competence, 95
  acquired, 96
project management methodology, 110
  preferred, 111

project managers, 110–111
  trained, 112
project process, 62, 99, 137, 142
projects, 44, 45, 54, 70, 71, 73, 79, 81, 87, 94–96, 102, 110–113, 118, 136, 137
  managing, 112, 113
  new, 89, 92, 93
  work teams, 92
prospective coaches, 63
psychology, 32

Q

quadrant, 128
questionnaire, 62, 71, 82, 84, 127, 134, 135, 136
  organisational, 73
  postprocess, 113

R

reaching agreement, 68, 77, 79, 107
recognition, 17, 38, 61, 120, 134
relationships, 6, 10, 15, 20, 33, 37, 38, 55, 80, 108, 120, 134
  improved, 109, 112
  special client-coach, 25
relevance, 28, 55, 56, 62, 82, 100, 106
renewal, 19, 24, 33
  organisational, 14
reorganisation, 30
research, 3, 50, 68, 86, 118, 123, 130, 134, 135, 136
  project, 54, 62, 63, 69, 94, 96
research process, 82, 120, 135
  complete, 134
resistance, 67, 95
resourcefulness, 61, 75, 76, 86, 129
resources, 59, 80, 108, 136, 145, 146–147
responses, 9, 16, 17, 29, 55, 67, 68, 81, 83, 84, 90
responsibility, 8, 9, 29, 31, 81, 83, 87, 88, 90–91, 93, 94, 112, 113, 118, 128
  client's, 26
  personal, 117, 126
role culture, 82, 83
  preferred, 82
role orientation, 83, 97, 102, 103, 104
roles, 1–2, 10, 11, 29, 30, 31, 61, 98, 117, 118, 119, 120, 124, 129, 131
  multiple, 131
  roles change, 118
  rules, 19, 83, 85, 92, 99

S

sales, 87, 89, 92, 94, 100
  processes, 87
sales strategy, 87, 88, 92, 96
  comprehensive, 87
Scandinavia, 3, 11, 43, 44
schools, 32, 39, 110
scope, 50, 133, 134
scores, 71, 72, 82, 119, 134
scripts, 16, 119
seasoned coach, 36
self-coaching, 8, 37
self-discovery, 5
service, 17, 23, 32, 35, 45, 49, 56, 61, 62, 85, 116
sessions, 31, 32, 33, 34, 35, 36, 66, 69, 71, 76, 78, 79, 118, 119, 123
  individual, 77, 86
  sensitising, 69, 70
shared values, 6, 11, 15, 17, 21, 24, 45, 59, 128
skilled coach, 7
skills, 3, 10, 27, 28, 30, 36, 37, 109, 111, 112, 116, 118, 126, 134, 136
  new, 27, 28, 30, 37, 44
solutions, 25, 27, 100, 108, 110, 124, 125, 131
  client-generated, 4, 5
  complete, 85, 99, 100
source, 16, 26, 28, 34, 36, 104, 108, 137
sponsors, 50, 112, 116, 136
staff, 17, 19, 48, 58, 59, 61, 80, 83, 85, 88, 89, 97, 102, 108, 111
staff members, 50, 62, 71, 82, 92, 93, 94, 98, 106, 134, 142
  individual, 91
  new, 96
stage of coaching, 32, 76
stakeholders, 16, 18–19, 21, 39, 45, 54, 65, 66, 67, 70, 107, 108, 109, 136, 137
standards, 10, 97
  ethical, 14, 59, 115, 117
state, 15, 24, 35, 37, 40, 44, 58, 100, 107, 110, 124
  desired, 34–35

mental, 116
preferred, 33, 35, 127
steps, 19, 54, 68, 70, 71, 72, 73, 82, 84, 86, 91, 92, 99, 106, 119
stories, 43, 124, 125
storytelling, 125
strategic objectives, 20, 139, 140–142
strategy, 4, 5, 15, 16, 18, 48, 53, 56, 58, 59, 69, 70, 96, 97, 132
  organisational, 68, 70, 77, 81, 94
style, 4, 5, 36, 59, 105
  coach's, 76
subconscious mind, 8
subcultures, 20
  aligned, 21
subject, 9, 14, 40, 69, 71, 115
subscribe, 115, 116
suppliers, 35, 58, 61, 66
supply chain, new, 44
supportive culture, strong, 98
survey, 53, 71, 72, 82, 101
  cultural, 53, 54
  organisational, 68, 82
sustain, 15, 16, 19, 20, 77, 101
sustainable long-term value, 43
Sweden, 43, 46, 102, 104
Swedish client/s, 26, 43
  message, 47
synergy, 14, 19, 21

T

teachers, 28, 39, 125
team alignment process, 105
team behaviours, 50, 72, 73, 84, 86
team coach, 35, 61, 117, 124, 127
team coaching, 4, 6, 24, 25, 33, 35, 36, 72–76, 86, 88, 89, 90, 127, 128, 129
  approach, 67, 128
  outcomes, 90
  projects, 117
  rounds of, 86, 87
  started, 25
  work, 11
team coaching day, 73, 74
  final, 78
team coaching sessions, 74, 75, 90, 93, 94, 97
  early, 100

final, 96
team culture, 19
team goals, 13, 50, 77, 134
team member efforts, 80
team members, 29, 30, 61, 71, 75, 76, 81, 83, 85, 87, 88, 90, 92, 93, 128
  enquiring, 74
  individual, 73, 76, 106
  teams, 3, 19, 35, 40, 50, 62, 67, 72, 75, 85–86, 90, 94, 95, 106–108, 118
  aligned, 40
  cohesive, 57
  cultural, 126
  diverse, 87
  engineering, 17
  inclusive, 88
  individual, 57
  management, 106
  working, 74
team values, 3, 23
teamwork, 30, 74, 80, 98, 100, 124
theory, 27, 58–59, 125
thinking, 9, 19, 23, 33, 34, 37, 43, 45, 46, 67, 108, 123, 124, 125, 129
  hats, 33, 35, 36
  organisation's, 72
third coaching cycle, 75
threats, 58–61, 92
tools, 4, 23, 49, 50, 60, 71, 93, 135
  market analysis, 58–59
trainer, 28, 29, 32, 44, 118, 124, 131, 134
training, 6, 7, 20, 24, 30, 44, 45, 49, 95, 109–111, 113
transcripts, 54, 81, 130
transformation, 1, 30, 37, 116, 117, 125
translation, 17, 68, 69
trust, 26, 31, 47, 66, 69, 103, 107, 130, 136, 137
turnover, 47, 139

U

uncomplicated business experience, 60, 139
understanding, 6, 44, 47, 66, 69, 79, 90, 116, 118, 125, 131, 134, 135, 137
units, project-oriented business, 92
unlearning, 67, 108
unstructured conversation, 128

V

value alignment, 56
value-based challenges, 16
value creation, 16
valued associates, 116
values, 6, 8, 11, 13–21, 23, 29, 48, 49, 55, 66, 117, 120, 132, 134, 135
  act, 15
  client's, 119
  coach's, 8
  collective, 3
  core, 15, 18
  corporate, 13, 15
  dominant, 63
  human, 13, 14
  key, 16, 49, 58
  minimal, 115
  organisation's, 20
  organisational, 21
  people's, 40
  selected, 16
  statement, 59
  term, 13
variances, 62, 72, 84, 86, 108
  significant, 72, 84–85
vehicle, 44, 49, 53, 69, 80, 117
viewpoints, 26, 39, 66, 67, 88
Viking Enterprises, 30, 41, 43–48, 50, 51, 53–56, 60–62, 65–68, 70, 74, 77, 79, 81, 85, 91, 99–105, 107, 109, 120, 126–127, 131, 133, 138, 144
  culture of, 48, 66, 102, 103, 104
  customer, 61
  essence, 104
  process, 104, 105
  pursued, 45
  smaller, 102
Viking organisation, 46
  subcultures, 45
  team members, 99
vision, 17, 65, 66, 67, 70, 81, 120, 128, 144
  common, 44, 45
  new, 24, 47, 49, 53, 70, 93, 96
  organisation's, 21

W

work culture, 20, 55
workplace, 3, 6, 15, 30, 109, 112, 113, 126
workshops, 56, 59, 61
  project training, 93
work teams, 3, 6, 30, 126
  natural, 29
  prospective, 29
  smaller, 74, 128
worldviews, 23, 25, 31

www.ingramcontent.com/pod-product-compliance
Lightning Source LLC
Chambersburg PA
CBHW080434230426
43662CB00015B/2270